MAMMAL TRACKS *and* SIGN *of the* NORTHEAST

MAMMAL TRACKS
and SIGN
of the NORTHEAST

Diane K. Gibbons

University Press of New England

HANOVER AND LONDON

Published by University Press of New England
One Court Street, Lebanon, NH 03766
www.upne.com

© 2003 by Diane K. Gibbons

All rights reserved. No part of this book may be
reproduced in any form or by any electronic or mechanical
means, including storage and retrieval systems, without
permission in writing from the publisher, except by a
reviewer, who may quote brief passages in a review.
Members of educational institutions and organizations
wishing to photocopy any of the work for classroom use,
or authors and publishers who would like to obtain
permission for any of the material in the work, should
contact Permissions, University Press of New England,
One Court Street, Lebanon, NH 03766.

Printed in the United States of America 5 4 3 2

LIBRARY OF CONGRESS CATALOGING-IN-PUBLICATION DATA

Gibbons, Diane.
Mammal tracks and sign of the Northeast
Diane Gibbons.
      p.   cm.
Includes bibliographical references (p.   ).
ISBN 1-58465-242-x (pbk. : alk. paper)
1. Animal tracks—Northeastern States. 2. Mammals—
Northeastern States—Identification. I. Title.
QL768 .G53 2003
599.1479—dc21   2002151142

Illustration of tracks, wildlife, and sign by Diane Gibbons
Cover art: Watercolors by September Vhay
           Tracks and pencil drawings by Diane Gibbons

Except for voles, shrews and Norway rats, all track
measurements are reprinted from *Tracking & the Art of
Seeing: How to Read Animal Tracks and Sign,* by Paul
Rezendes © 1999 by Paul Rezendes, Second Edition,
Harper Perennial, a division of HarperCollins Publishers,
Inc. All rights reserved. Used by permission of the author.

For Sarah—

May the love of animals

always be a magical part

of your days on earth . . .

Contents

Acknowledgments   ix

Introduction   1
   Method of Devising the Key and Manual   3
     Using the Key   4
     Definitions of Terms   5
     Gaits and Corresponding Track Patterns   7
   A Key to the Mammal Tracks of the Northeast   11
Compression Shapes   15

MAMMALS OF THE NORTHEAST

Species Listed in Order:

Family	*Species*	
Didelphidae	Virginia Opossum	18
Soricidae	Shrews	20
Leporidae	Cottontail, Eastern and New England	22
	Snowshoe Hare	24
Sciuridae	Eastern Chipmunk	26
	Woodchuck	28
	Gray Squirrel	30
	Red Squirrel	32
	Flying Squirrel, Northern and Southern	34

Castoridae	Beaver	36
Muridae	Deer Mouse and White-Footed Mouse	40
	Voles	42
	Muskrat	44
Murinae	Norway Rat	46
Zapodidae	Meadow Jumping Mouse and Woodland Jumping Mouse	48
Erethizontidae	Porcupine	50
Canidae	Domestic Dog	52
	Gray Wolf	54
	Coyote	58
	Red Fox	60
	Gray Fox	64
Ursidae	Black Bear	66
Procyonidae	Raccoon	70
Mustelidae	Weasels, Long-tailed, Short-tailed, and Least	72
	Mink	74
	Marten	76
	Fisher	80
	River Otter	82
Mephitidae	Striped Skunk	86
Felidae	Housecat	88
	Bobcat	90
	Lynx	92
	Mountain Lion	96
Cervidae	White-tailed Deer	100
	Elk or Wapiti	104
	Moose	106

Comparison Pages	109
Breeding Seasons in the Northeast	128
Notes	131
Bibliography	133
Index	135

Acknowledgments

In tracking my own process of putting together this book, I realized that a tremendous number of individuals have been involved. My deepest gratitude to Tom Brown, Jr., who introduced me to the joy of tracking through his writings and classes; Paul Rezendes, for his great knowledge of the wild ones, for his impeccable measurements, which are used throughout this book, and for his and his wife Paulette's friendship; Susan Morse for her warm support and her willingness to share her information and images of wild cat tracks, and for all she does to preserve wild habitat through Keeping Track; Jon Young and the Kamana Program; Patti Smith, for her artistic suggestions; my tracking partner, Linda Spielman, for all she has taught me of the natural world, especially her information related to the mustelids; Sue Mansfield and Al Stoops, for teaching me so much about black bear and for all our times together wandering quietly in the woods; Joe Merritt of Powdermill Biological Station in Rector, Pennsylvania, for his help livetrapping small mammals in order to get their tracks; Sue McLaren of the Carnegie Museum's Mammal Collection; Michaele Glennon, for her tracks of small mammals; Roger Powell of the University of North Carolina and Steve Buskirk of the University of Wyoming; Jon Atwood and Tom Wessels at Antioch New England Graduate School for their immense patience, knowledge, and support; Glenn and Kathy Eldridge, directors of Greenville Wildlife Park in Greenville, New Hampshire, for helping me obtain photos of lynx and mountain lion tracks; my dear friends Gail Schmick, Barbara Atwood and Beth Bannister; Ann Stokes, for her support, friendship, and a beautiful place to live and write for a couple of years; Meade Cadot, for his guidance, his enthusiasm for wildlife, his undying commitment to protecting wildland habitat, and for always being available for my questions; Helen Whybrow, editor, friend, and handholder par excellence; Doug Lufkin, for his great rangemap work; the terrific people of University Press of New England, who have been wonderful to work with; my husband Paul, who never ceases to nurture me on my path and who is the most amazing husband in the whole world; my mother, who made sure this dream stayed alive, and my father, who first sat me down in front of Wild Kingdom so many years ago and said "Look at how that cat moves!" thus beginning my abiding love for animals and tracking; to all my friends, who have put up with me while I worked on this book—you know who you are; Jasmine, Camo, Pilgrim, and Bumpkin, for what they have taught me of domestic animals and for being quiet companions and family; and to those who have been my tracking teachers in spirit through their art and writing—Olas Murie, Ernest Thompson Seton, and Henry David Thoreau.

Most especially, I'd like to thank my tracking and drawing mentor, Charles Worsham, who taught me to *see* tracks in both their inner and outer dimensions, who taught me how to take what I was seeing and put it onto paper, and who has for many years been both a great teacher and friend. Much of the information in this book as well as the skill of drawing tracks has come from Charles's patient teaching, encouragement, and inspiration.

And finally, my deepest gratitude to the Wild Ones, the greatest tracking teachers of all, for the immense richness they have added to my life.

D.K.G.

MAMMAL TRACKS *and* SIGN *of the* NORTHEAST

Introduction

I tread in the steps of the fox that has gone before me by some hours . . . I am curious to know what has determined its graceful curvatures, and how surely they were coincident with the fluctuations of some mind. I know which way a mind wended, what horizon it faced, by the setting of these tracks, and whether it moved slowly or rapidly, by their greater or less intervals and distinctness; for the swiftest step leaves yet a lasting trace.
—HENRY DAVID THOREAU "The Natural History of Massachusetts."

In the past fifteen years or so, animal tracking has been rediscovered as a popular tool for understanding wildlife. Nature centers, tracking schools, and nature-focused organizations have added workshops and classes on animal tracking to their itineraries. Once the domain of hunters and a few field biologists, tracking has become the pastime and passion of an increasing number of people who want to understand more about wild animals.

What is it about tracking that is so much fun? First of all, it is a detective game. In order to identify the maker of a set of tracks, you need to look carefully and search for both obvious and subtle clues. There is immense satisfaction in making a positive identification of a difficult set of tracks. When you figure out the identification of a species you can backtrack and learn what the animal did. You can connect with the personality and drama of this particular animal as you figure out how it spent a segment of time. Once, wandering down by a small stream in New York state, I found a great many tracks surrounding an old plastic milk jug. The tracks told me that a bunch of coyotes had had a good time the night before playing on the ice, skidding around and biting on the milk jug, playing a kind of coyote hockey! Another time in southern New Hampshire I was following the trail of a bull moose and came to a place where he had thrashed every tree in a small area, biting and walking over several of them. The moose was in rut (not a great time to encounter one, incidentally) and full of testosterone. His way of dealing with his hormones at that moment was to beat up on a whole bunch of trees. Furthermore, the tree breakage and tracks were recent. I knew that a moose full of that much energy and frustration was a moose to leave alone, so I left the area. Knowing how to read the tracks and sign helped keep me safe but also gave me insight into this particular animal's life in that moment—his desires and frustrations and how he expressed them. I have learned many things about animals and their lives from reading the stories in their tracks.

Tracking is a science, an art, and a skill that you never perfect but can continue to learn. Once you've learned to identify basic tracks, you can learn to age them, and to track in different, and increasingly more difficult, substrates. You can learn sign tracking to supplement footprint tracking, looking for claw marks, scat, kills, dens, and other such markings and leavings of animals.

Tracking on an advanced level is a wildlife biologist's essential tool and can open up a whole new world for the naturalist. By exploring tracks you can learn more about predator/prey interactions, breeding activity, the behavior of different species, and life and death in the wild. You can become woven into the community of animals that share a particular locale, learning who the individuals are by carefully studying their tracks and then mapping their travels, behaviors, and interactions with other animals of that location.

Tracking allows you to "touch" wildlife in non-intrusive ways and can be a deeply spiritual and aesthetic experience as well. By challenging you to develop your awareness in order to see what are sometimes very subtle clues on the landscape, tracking can connect you to the wild world in unexpected ways. One warm winter day I spent a long time just sitting by a stream enjoying the beauty of a set of mink tracks rhythmically undulating down the side of the bank. I was deeply moved by these tracks, and when I finally looked up from them and turned in the other direction, there was the mink herself looking at me! We stared at each other for what seemed to be a long time, and then she was off down the river again. I felt that our separate worlds had momentarily opened to one another in a deep and magical way.

Most of us today don't have the luxury of learning to track over many years beside a master tracker, and we have to use books to supplement our training. Taking workshops, classes, and apprenticeships is a good idea, but at some point it comes down to you and the track, and that is where a good manual or field guide helps. While there are many tracking books available to hobby trackers and field biologists, all have their limitations. One of the great limitations of many of them is the wealth of material that one has to look through to find precise tracking information. Natural history about various species and anecdotal information make the reading very interesting, but a tracker has to sort through all this information to get a positive identification in the field. At the other end of the spectrum are books on tracking that are too simplistic to be of great use to biologists or more advanced trackers, who need precision in identification.

This field guide is unique in several respects. First of all, it begins with a dichotomous key that leads the tracker or biologist through a process of looking at the track and finding the most precise details that define its maker. Dichotomous keys are most commonly used for identifying plants and trees but are a simple way of working toward a positive identification of anything that has a reliable structure or pattern to it, which tracks have. The key leads to the species pages, which have very detailed drawings of front and rear tracks, including notes detailing the set of features of the tracks that are unique to that species. The track illustrations in all of the examples are drawn to their natural size, which also helps in identification.

Overall, I have designed this field guide to be simple, easy to use, and yet very detailed in the rendition of the tracks themselves.

Like other tracking books, this field guide has its limitations. The key is most useful for working with clear prints where toes and pads are distinguishable. Most tracks you find will have only some of the aspects presented in the drawing. But presenting all of what might be there gives the biologist or tracker more to look for, even in partial tracks. When you find the trail of an animal you want to identify, it is best to follow the trail for a while and look at many tracks, examining each of them to create a composite idea of the elements found in them. Also, mud, sand, and snow are the substrates where you will find the clearest prints. If you are tracking an animal that has unclear prints, you can try to backtrack it until you find where it crossed a bit of mud or sand, for instance, or you can look for a clear snow track.

This work is the culmination of ten years of serious study of animal tracking and drawing. I hope that it will become a useful tool for both the beginning tracker and the professional. I further hope it may play a role in working to understand and protect the wild mammal species of our region.

Method of Devising the Key and Manual

There are six different physical aspects of tracks used in identification: overall shape, size, details within the track (number of toes, shape of pads, relation of toes to each other, etc.), gait pattern, habitat, and other sign near where the tracks are found. This manual deals with all of these aspects on the species pages. In devising this key, however, the most important distinguishing characteristic of a species' track was selected, so that by a process of elimination you can identify which mammal track you are probably looking at.

The tracks illustrated on the species pages are composite drawings of all the elements that you may find in a track. For devising these composite drawings I used my own extensive tracking log with drawings and photographs, as well as photographs from Paul Rezende's *Tracking & the Art of Seeing: How to Read Animal Tracks and Sign,* and drawings from Olaus Murie's book *A Field Guide to Animal Tracks.* Wild lynx and mountain lion information and photos used to render their illustrations were given to me by wildlife tracker and felid expert Susan Morse. These supplemented my own photos of captive lynx and mountain lion tracks.

Most of the information on track sizes and trail width is taken from Paul Rezende's *Tracking & the Art of Seeing.* While I do take measurements in the field, Paul has made a much longer and more in-depth study of track measurements. The exceptions are the trail widths on shrews and voles, which were taken from my own measurements.

Some species in this book are rare or endangered and have limited populations or ranges. These include the marten, New England cottontail, and lynx. While it is believed the Eastern wolf and the mountain lion do not have breeding populations in the Northeastern United States, some sightings of these animals have occurred, and so I have included them. I do not include the handful of introduced species with extremely limited ranges such as the black-tailed jackrabbit and the European wild boar, nor do I cover coastal mammals such as seals.

Using the Key

Remember that this key, which appears on page 11, is easiest to use with clear prints (or with trail width, as in the cases of weasels and small mammals), and is more of a challenge to use with partial or unclear prints. You are going to have two options at each identification decision and will identify the track through a process of elimination. Let me give you an example:

When you have a reasonably clear track for identification, start at the beginning of the key (1A and 1B). Determine whether the print has two toes or more. For example, say you have found a track with what appears to be four toes. You would go to 1B, "Tracks have more than two toes," which then takes you to 4A and 4B. Here you need to determine if the animal has four toes on all four feet, or whether it has more on some or all of its feet. In our example, you look and see that it has 4 toes on all the tracks you can see. (It is best, by the way, to look at a number of prints before determining the number of toes, as well as prints where there are gait changes, since toes may not appear on one given print or in one gait pattern, and you will wind up making a wrong identification.)

Since your animal has 4 toes on all 4 feet, you would go to number 5 and decide on the overall shape of the track, round (5A) or oblong (5B). Your track is oblong, so you go to number 10. Here you have to look for two things: size and a detail of the track that will or will not show in the plantar pad of the front foot, namely a bar or chevron. You measure the track and find that it is longer than 2 ⅞ inches, and it doesn't have the bar or chevron in the front track, which eliminates 10A. You go to 10B, which leads you to number 11. Here you are directed to the size again, but more importantly, to the placement of the toes. On your track you notice that the toes are held tightly together, and the measurements fit, so you go to the species page for coyote. On the species page you look for more specific details that help confirm your identification. Your four-toed, oblong track with no bar or chevron does indeed have a pointed plantar pad, a mound in the middle, and an X can be drawn through it. You have the track of a coyote in front of you!

If you are unsure of your identification, check the "Comparisons" area on the species page, if there is one. There you will find other species that have similar tracks that are easily confused with the one on that page. In the case of the coyote, this would be the red fox, domestic dog, and wolf. Keep in mind that it is best to look at several tracks of the same animal when determining identification.

Finally, I have included trail width, habitat, food sources, scat and urine, breeding times, and special clues on the species pages to help support a positive identification, and to help you understand information in and around the tracks.

Other Things to Keep in Mind When Using this Field Guide

- When looking at gait pattern illustrations, the front tracks are light, while the rear tracks are dark.
- All tracks illustrated are of the left feet of the species, unless all four are drawn.
- Tracks and scat are drawn to actual size unless indicated.
- Scat is highly variable due to changes in diet, and the illustrations indicate only one or two forms of the scat that you might find of each animal.

Definitions of Terms

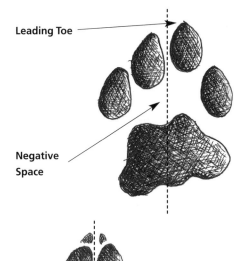

Leading Toe

Negative Space

Asymmetry, Symmetry, and Negative Space
This print from the felid, or cat, family is an **asymmetrical** print, meaning that if you drew a line down the middle of the track, the sides would be different from each other. The cat family shows a leading toe on the front track, and the heel pad cants outward, which creates the asymmetry.

The space where there is no toe or heel impression is referred to as **negative space**. The measurement of negative space is helpful in determining front from rear feet and one species from another.

This print from the canid family is a **symmetrical** print, meaning that if you drew a line down the middle of the track, both sides would be pretty much the same.

Bar   Chevron

Bar or Chevron
In the plantar pad of the red fox, there is a straight bar or chevron.

Cat doing direct register walk

Direct and Indirect Register
An animal that places its hind foot directly into the track made by its front foot is doing a **direct register,** while one that

Cat doing indirect register walk

steps to the outside, only partly within, behind, or forward of the front track is doing an **indirect register**.

Humanlike Prints
Prints like this one of the black bear are **humanlike,** meaning that the overall shape resembles a human footprint. It has five toes, a plantar pad similar to the ball of our foot, and the heel may register.

Pads
Toe pads are located at the tip of the toes, and sometimes the track will only show the compression of the toe pads rather than the whole toe, as in this skunk track. The pads located at the base of the toes are called **plantar pads.** Some animals have another pad or set of pads that corresponds to the metacarpal or carpal bones of the feet. These may be referred to as **heel pads,** metacarpal pads, carpal pads, or proximal pads. Though technically not correct in all cases, they are referred to in this guide as **heel pads** for ease of comparison.

Stride
The **stride** is the measurement from one track on one side of the body to the next placement of the same foot's track. **Half strides** (or steps) are from one front track on one side to the next front track on the other side, or from one rear track on one side to the next rear track on the other side.

Stride on walk

Half Stride

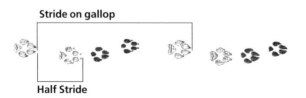

Stride on gallop

Half Stride

Trail Width

Trail width, also referred to in other tracking books as "straddle," is the distance from the outside of the right track to the outside of the left track. In groups of four prints, such as jumps, bounds, and gallops, trail width is measured from the outside of the outermost tracks.

Trail width measurement:

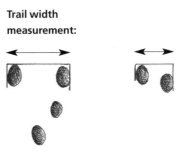

Vestigial Toes and Dewclaws

In the course of evolution, some animals had toes that disappeared over time. **Vestigial toes** are toes that are thought to be in the process of disappearing. Vestigial toes are smaller than other toes and only show up in tracks occasionally. **Dewclaws** are vestigial toes that sit higher up on the back part of the foot. Dewclaws only show sometimes in a track. Canids, felids, and ungulates have dewclaws.

Vestigal toe

Dewclaws

Gaits and Corresponding Track Patterns

Understanding gaits and track patterns and what they reveal is a whole study in itself and therefore is not covered in detail here. What follows is a simplified explanation. Track patterns can indicate species, even if you don't have a clear print. Track patterns can also indicate whether an animal is hunting, playing, running from a predator, and so forth. For more in-depth examination of gaits, please refer to gait references in the bibliography.

Gaits: Walk, trot, or pace.

Track Pattern: Randomly or evenly spaced alternating tracks, or evenly spaced coupled tracks. In a **walking gait,** the footfall sequence is front, rear, front, rear, in a four-beat pattern. The rear foot following the front can either be on the same side of the body as the front, or the opposite side. For example, if a cat starts with the right front foot, it will likely follow with a left rear, then left front, then right rear. If it is indirect registering, it will leave a pattern like this:

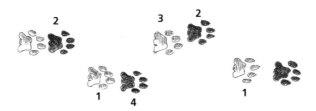

front rear

An animal doing a walking gait can leave evenly spaced tracks or randomly spaced tracks, such as when it is wandering around or checking something out. In a **trotting gait** the front foot on one side of the body moves at the same time as the rear foot on the opposite side of the body, making a two-beat pattern. When an animal **paces,** the front and rear foot on the same side of the body move more or less at the same time.

It is often hard to tell if an animal is walking, trotting, or pacing, due to the fact that the track patterns on the ground can look similar. What differentiates them are two measurements. First, **trail width** changes when speed changes. It narrows when an animal goes into a trot and widens when it walks. Second, **stride** changes as well, lengthening as an animal moves from a walk to a trot and shortening as it slows to a walk. The best way to tell the gait an animal is using is to follow it out until you find a place where the trail width and stride changes.

Cat doing Direct Register Walk
Trail width wider, stride shorter

Cat doing Indirect Register Trot
Trail width narrower, stride longer

A common gait unique to the canids that leaves a pattern of evenly spaced coupled tracks is the oblique trot. In the oblique trot the posterior of the body is thrown out at an angle, which makes the rear feet fall to one side of the front feet.

Oblique Trot

Gaits: Lope, gallop, jump.

Track Pattern: Groups of 4 tracks, or what appears to be 3 tracks. The track pattern of the **lope** is different from the actual footfall of the gait itself. In the gait itself the footfall is most often front, front, rear, rear, which creates a rolling or rocking movement. However, the visual track pattern is clearly front, rear, front, rear. This is because the first rear foot to land hits the ground behind where the leading front foot has landed.

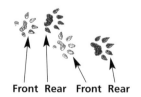

Front   Rear   Front   Rear

When the first rear foot lands on top of the leading front track, the visual track pattern looks more like a pattern of three tracks, though it is really four.

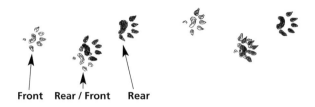

Front   Rear / Front   Rear

In the **galloping** gait each foot lands at a different time, with the rear feet coming around the body and landing ahead of the front feet. The track pattern appears as a group of four tracks, the order being front, front, rear, rear. Both the front and rear tracks are set at a sharp angle, which distinguishes it from the jump.

Gallop

In the **jumping** gait the front feet land side by side or at an angle to one another and the rear feet come around the body to land ahead of the front feet. The rear tracks in a jump appear parallel to each other, or only slightly angled. The track pattern appears as a group of four with the front feet falling behind and inside the rear feet, and with the rear feet nearly directly across from each other. This gait is particularly common for rodents, rabbits, and hares, though other species will also jump.

Jump

Gait: **Bound.**

Track Pattern: 2 pairs of direct register compressions, side by side, or 2 compressions with 2 more compressions close behind. In the **bounding** gait the front feet hit the ground at the same time, or nearly the same time, and the rear feet are brought up under the body and fall directly into, or just behind, the front tracks. Visually it can look like two tracks side by side, but actually there are four tracks tightly grouped or superimposed. This gait is particularly common for the smaller and larger weasels.

Bound

Measuring Tracks

Measuring individual tracks can be highly technical or very general depending upon your purpose for measuring. For most trackers the basic measurement of track length and width of the track is sufficient. For stricter scientific purposes, internal measurements of toes, plantar, and heel pad lengths and widths, and the distances between pads or between toes and claws, all provide greater accuracy. Such measurements can also be useful in identifying individual animals. Measuring the negative space between the toes and the plantar or heel pads, or the distance from toes to dewclaws on ungulates, can help to determine front from rear feet. In terms of claws or nails, different trackers measure differently, some including them in measurements and others excluding them. While there are good arguments for both practices, for the purposes of this book they are included.

A Key to the Mammal Tracks of the Northeast

See page 4 for a guide for using this key.

1A. Tracks have two toes **2**

1B. Tracks have more than two toes **4**

2A. Toes are kidney-shaped . . . . **Elk** page 104

2B. Toes form a heart-shaped track **3**

3A. Toes are blunt, track is usually over 4 in. (10.2 cm) long
. . . . **Moose (adult)** page 106

3B. Toes are pointy, track is usually under 4 in. (10.2 cm) long
. . . . **White-tailed deer** page 100

4A. Tracks in a group have four toes on all four feet **5**

4B. Tracks in a group have some feet, or all feet, with
more than 4 toes **13**

5A. Tracks are round or nearly round **6**

5B. Tracks are oblong **10**

6A. Plantar pad on front is shallow with round leading edge
. . . . **Gray fox** page 64

6B. Plantar pad is not shallow with round leading edge. **7**

7A. Tracks are less than 3 in. (7.6 cm) long **8**

7B. Tracks are 3 in. (7.6 cm) or longer. **9**

8A. Tracks are less than 1 ⅞ in. (4.8 cm) long . . . . **Housecat** page 88

8B. Tracks are between 1 ⅞ in. (4.8 cm) and 2 ½ in.
(6.4 cm) long . . . . **Bobcat** page 90

front rear

9A. Toes appear tiny in relation to overall track . . . . **Lynx** page 92

9B. Toes appear large in relation to overall track. . . . **Mountain lion** page 96

10A. Track is between 2 ⅛ in. (5.4 cm) and 2 ⅞ in. (7.3 cm) long
and has a chevron or bar in front plantar pad. . . . . **Red fox** page 60

10B. Track does not have a chevron or bar in front plantar pad. **11**

11A. Track is between 2 ⅞ in. (7.3 cm) and 3 ½ in. (8.9 cm) long,
and all toes are tightly held together . . . . **Coyote** page 58

11B. Outer toes are splayed out **12**

12A. Middle toes are parallel . . . . **Gray wolf** page 54

12B. Middle toes are spread, and track is very splayed out
. . . . **Domestic dog** page 52

13A. Front and rear tracks have different numbers of toes **14**

13B. Front and rear tracks have 5 toes **26**

14A. Front track has 5 toes and rear track has 4 toes **15**

14B. Front track has 4 toes (sometime with a vestigial thumb) and
rear track has 5 toes. **16**

15A. Rear track is less than 1 ½ in. (3.8 cm) wide
. . . . **Eastern or New England cottontail** page 22

15B. Rear track is greater than 1 ½ in. (3.8 cm) wide . **Snowshoe hare** page 24

16A. Tracks appear humanlike with a long nubby heel pad **Porcupine** page 50

16B. Tracks do not appear humanlike at all **17**

17A. Tracks have a heart-shaped plantar pad . . . . **Woodchuck** page 28

17B. Tracks do not have a heart-shaped plantar pad **18**

18A. Tracks are found going completely in and out of water **19**

18B. Tracks are not found going completely in and out of water **20**

19A. Rear track is 3 in. (7.6 cm) or less . . . . **Muskrat** page 44

19B. Rear track is 4 in. (10.2 cm) or more . . . . **Beaver** page 36

20A. Tracks have outer toes directly or nearly directly across
from each other . . . . **Norway rat** page 46

20B. Tracks do not have outer toes directly or nearly directly across
from each other **21**

21A. Tracks are found in fields or woodlands, often in consistent
groups of 4 (indicating jumps) **22**

21B. Tracks are found in fields or woodlands, but track pattern tends
to be shuffling walk rather than consistent jumps. . . . . **Voles** page 42

22A. Smaller front tracks frequently appear ahead of or between
larger rear tracks . . . . **Flying squirrels** page 34

22B. Smaller front tracks appear behind or between larger rear tracks **23**

23A. The overall track group has a trail width less than 1 ¾ in.
(4.4 cm) . . . . **Mice spp. and Jumping mice** page 40 and page 48

23B. The overall track group has a trail width over 1 ¾ in. (4.4 cm) **24**

24A. The overall track group has a trail width between 2 ⅛ in. (5.4 cm)
and 3 ⅛ in. (7.9 cm) . . . . **Eastern chipmunk** page 26

24B. The overall track group has a trail width between 3 in. (7.6 cm)
and 6 in. (15.2 cm) **25**

25A. Overall track group is between 3 in. (7.6 cm) and 4 ¼ in. (10.8cm)
and is found close to conifers. . . . . **Red squirrel** page 32

25B. Overall track group is between 3 ½ in. (8.9 cm) and 6 in. (15.2 cm)
and is near deciduous trees . . . . **Gray squirrel** page 30

26A. Tracks are greater than 5 in. (12.7 cm) long and humanlike
. . . . **Black bear** page 66

26B. Tracks are less than 5 in. (12.7 cm) long **27**

27A. Tracks have an opposable toe on front and rear, with rear track often cradling front track . . . . **Virginia opossum** page 18

27B. Tracks do not have an opposable toe on front and rear **28**

28A. Tracks are in tiny runways under 1 ¼ in. (3.2 cm) wide. . **Shrews** page 20

28B. Tracks are not in tiny runways. **29**

29A. Tracks have a C-shaped plantar pad with long chubby fingers
. . . . **Raccoon** page 70

29B. Tracks do not have a C-shaped plantar pad with long chubby fingers. **30**

30A. Tracks appear humanlike and delicate and are small, to 2 ³⁄₁₆ in (5.6 cm) long . . . . **Striped skunk** page 86

30B. Tracks do not appear humanlike at all **31**

31A. Tracks are under 1 in. (2.5 cm) long and are in a
bounding pattern. . . . . **Weasels** page 72

31B. Tracks are over 1 in. (2.5 cm) long **32**

32A. Tracks are between 1 ¼ in. (3.2 cm) and 2 in (5.1 cm) long, are longer when the heel pad shows, and are found by water. . . . . **Mink** page 74
or in the far north in unbroken forests . . . . **Marten** page 76

32B. Tracks are over 2 in. (5.1 cm) long **33**

33A. Tracks are webbed with teardrop-shaped toes . . . . . . **River otter** page 82

33B. Tracks are not webbed and often show oblong toes . . . . . **Fisher** page 80

Compression Shapes

 Deer, Elk, Moose

Rabbits, Hares

 Dog, Wolf, Coyote, Foxes

Mice, Voles, Chipmunks, Squirrels

 Housecat, Bobcat, Lynx, Mountain Lion

Shrews, Voles

 Porcupine

Weasels, Mink, Fishers, Marten, Otter

 Bear, Skunk

Raccoon

 Beaver, Muskrat

 Virginia Opossum

 front rear

MAMMALS *of the* NORTHEAST

VIRGINIA OPOSSUM, *Didelphis virginiana*

Overall Track

- In good snow or mud, the plantar pads show prominently.
- Often the opossum's front track is cradled by the rear.
- This is a very distinctive track, not easily confused with other species.

Front Track

Often shows as a star pattern with the outside toes across from each other.

Size: 1½ to 2 ⅛ in. (3.8 to 5.4 cm) long; 1 ¾ to 2 ⅜ in. (4.4 to 6 cm) wide

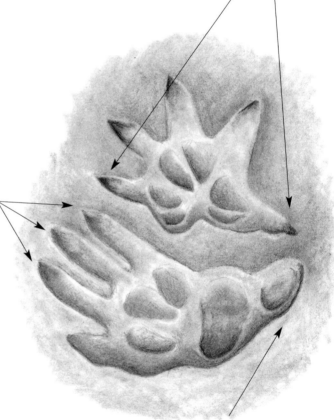

Rear Track

These three toes are longer than the outside toe and are often close to and parallel to one another.

Size: 1 ¾ to 2 ¾ in. (4.4 to 7 cm) long; 1 ¾ to 2 ⅞ in. (4.4 to 7.3 cm) wide

Look for the opposable thumb, which is especially clear in the rear track. This toe has no nail on it.

Virginia opossum clues:

Look for the cradled track, with the opposable thumb prominent on the rear track. Opossums are not real hibernators, but they do become less active in winter. There may be a narrow tail drag in the trail.

Trail width: 2 ½ to 4 ⅝ in. (6.4 to 11.7 cm)

Habitat: Highly adaptable. Inhabits forests, agricultural land, urban and suburban areas. Dens in hollow logs, brush piles, tree cavities, under buildings, and in other animals' abandoned dens.

Food: Omnivorous. Often forages along small streams. Insects, small mammals, green vegetation, fruits and berries, garbage, earthworms, amphibians, carrion.

Scat: Scat is variable and indistinguishable from many other mammals due to the variety of diet.

Breeding: February to June.

Walk:

front rear

SHREWS, *Sorex spp.* and *Blarina*

Overall Track

- Shrews have 5 toes on both front and back feet, unlike mice or voles.
- Shrews usually walk rather than jump, and their trail appears as a runway in the snow.

Front Track

Rear Track

Walking trail in snow: 1 in. (2.5 cm) wide or less. Will also jump.

Food: All shrews are voracious carnivores and eat worms and insects. The Northern short-tailed shrew is larger than other terrestrial shrew species and will also eat small mammals.

Scat: Tiny ovals.

Comparisons: Similar to mice and voles (page 109).

Shrew clues:

Look for small shallow, narrow tunnels in the snow. While most shrews use tunnels made by other small mammals, the Northern short-tailed shrew will dig its own tunnels.

Northern Short-tailed Shrew, *Blarina brevicauda*

Trail width: 1 in. (2.5 cm)

Habitat: Damp areas in forested or open habitat. Along stream banks, stone walls, in meadows with tall grasses, brush piles. Prefers hardwoods to softwoods.

Water Shrew, *Sorex palustris*

Trail width: 1 in. (2.5 cm)*

Habitat: This is a semi-aquatic shrew, and it can be found in wet areas near water bodies, especially shrubby areas along streams and ponds in conifer forests, beaver flowages, marshes, and wooded shore areas with cover. Also found away from water. Water shrews have hairs along their toes and feet that aid in swimming.

Smoky Shrew, *Sorex fumeus*

Trail width: ¾ in. (1.9 cm)*

Habitat: Damp areas of deciduous and coniferous forests containing boulder fields, with lots of leaf mold and decaying logs. Can also be found in clear-cuts, bogs, and swamps.

Masked Shrew, *Sorex cinereus*

Trail width: ⅝ in. (1.6 cm)*

Habitat: Damp woods with cover, bogs, clearcuts with debris.

Pygmy Shrew, *Sorex hoyi*

Trail width: ½ in. (1.3 cm)*

Habitat: Damp habitats near water.

*Note: Shrew trail widths marked with an asterisk are based on study skin measurements.

front rear

COTTONTAIL, EASTERN, *Sylvilagus floridanus,* and NEW ENGLAND, *Sylvilagus transitionalis*

Overall Track

- Cottontail tracks are asymmetrical.
- These tracks can be highly variable.
- One feature of hare and rabbit tracks is the pattern: they most often jump, leaving a set of four tracks with the larger rear tracks ahead, and outside of, the front tracks, with the front tracks placed one behind the other.
- Toe pads often do not show because the bottom of the foot is covered with fur.

Front Track

5 toes on the front.

Size: Less than 1 ¼ in. (3.2 cm) wide

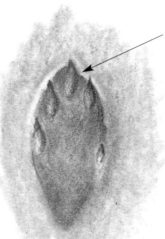

Look for this angled notch near the top, which appears on the inside of the track.

Variations of cottontail tracks

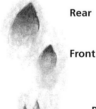

Rear

Front

Rear

Front

Rear Track

4 toes on the rear.

Size: Less than 1 ½ in. (3.8 cm) wide

Comparisons: Similar to snowshoe hare (page 110); squirrels (page 112).

Eastern and New England Cottontails

These two species are very similar in size and appearance. The Eastern cottontail is common, whereas only isolated populations remain of the New England cottontail.

Habitat: Eastern cottontails are highly adaptable, inhabiting residential areas, farmlands, thickets, and swampy woods. They need areas of cover for escape interspersed with grassy areas. They are rarely found in heavy forests. New England cottontails prefer areas of dense shrubbery.

Cottontail clues:

Look for "forms," which are shallow depressions in the ground in thickets and brushy areas where the rabbits sleep and nest. They will use woodchuck dens in the ground for shelter in winter but do not dig deep holes. Also look for 45-degree cuts on blueberry bushes and other small shrubs, and debarking on fruit trees. Cottontails use obvious trails in shrubs and grasses and make dust bath depressions about a foot in diameter.

Food: Wide variety of green foods in spring and summer. Winter foods include buds, twigs, the bark of trees and shrubs, and canes of the *rubus* species.

Scat: Scat are round pellets that look similar to snowshoe hare.

Breeding: February through September. Prolific breeders.

Jump: The rear feet fall ahead of the front feet.

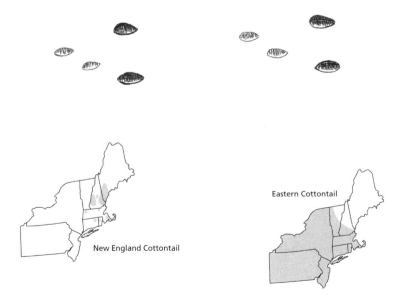

New England Cottontail

Eastern Cottontail

front rear

SNOWSHOE HARE, *Lepus americanus*

Overall Track

- Snowshoe hare tracks are asymmetrical.
- Look for a much larger rear track that looks like a snowshoe.
- Hares have very furry feet, so it is unusual to find distinct toe prints in the track.
- One feature of hare and rabbit tracks is the pattern: they most often jump, leaving a set of four tracks with the larger rear tracks ahead, and outside of, the front tracks, and with the front tracks placed one behind the other.
- Tracks can also appear narrow and very similar to a cottontail's track. Measure carefully and check habitat as an indicator.

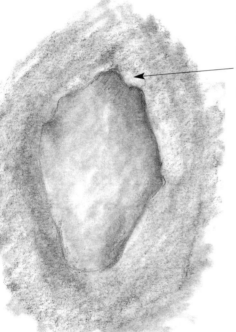

Front Track

4 toes on the front, though these rarely show. Look for this angled notch near the top, which appears on the inside of the track.

Size: 1 ¼ in. (3.2 cm) wide, or more

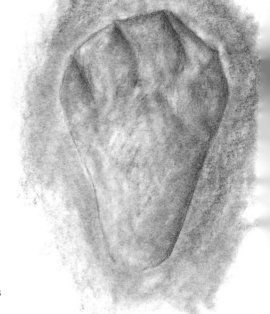

Rear Track

5 toes on the rear, which often appear very spread out, like a snowshoe. This is most often seen in snow.

Size: 1 ½ to 4 ½ in. (3.8 to 11.4 cm) wide

Comparisons: Similar to cottontail rabbits (page 110); and squirrels (page 112).

Trail width: Approximately 4 ¾ to 6 ½ in. (12.1 to 16.5 cm)

Habitat: Forest and brushy, semi-open areas surrounded by conifers. Needs some shrubby area for browse, and conifer saplings for cover. Also found in wetlands.

Food: Summer foods include grasses and herbaceous plants such as clover, vetch, and ferns, as well as buds and young leaves of woody plants like hazel, alder, and birch. Winter foods include twigs and buds of birches, sugar maple, quaking aspen, red and white pine, beaked hazelnut, and hemlock. The snowshoe hare eats a wide diversity of vegetation. This is not a complete list.

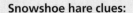

Snowshoe hare clues:

Look for 45-degree cuts on low bushes and hemlock saplings, as well as white pine, spruce, and young hardwoods, and for browse on accessible fruit tree branches. Lay areas are called "forms" and are made under conifers or in brush or thickets. Hares can leap long distances. Fur turns white in winter, brown in spring.

Scat and urine: Scat are small round pellets, similar to cottontails, that may be hard, or soft and covered with mucous. During winter scat appear very fibrous and woody. Urine may be found in the snow in trail. If it is sprayed out, it may be part of a courtship display.

Breeding: March or April through early August.

Jump:

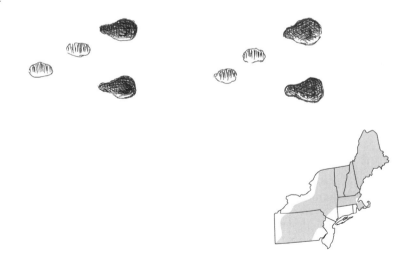

EASTERN CHIPMUNK, *Tamias striatus*

Overall Track

- Measuring trail width is the best way to determine the species of smaller mammals.
- Rear tracks most often appear ahead of the front tracks in the common jumping pattern.

Rear Tracks (Top)

5 toes on the rear.

Size: ½ to ¾ in. (1.3 to 1.9 cm) long; ⅝ to ¹⁵⁄₁₆ in. (1.6 to 2.4 cm) wide.

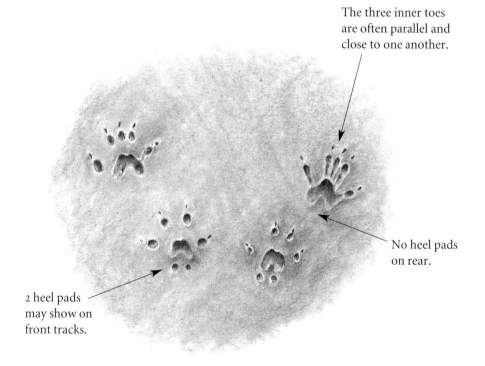

The three inner toes are often parallel and close to one another.

No heel pads on rear.

2 heel pads may show on front tracks.

Front Tracks (Bottom)

4 toes on the front.
A vestigial thumb may occasionally show on the inside.

Size: ⅞ to 1 in. (2.2 to 2.5 cm) long; ⁷⁄₁₆ to ¹³⁄₁₆ in. (1.1 to 2.1 cm) wide

Comparisons: Similar to squirrels, mice, and voles (page 111).

Trail width: 2 ⅛ to 3 ⅛ in. (5.4 to 7.9 cm)

Habitat: Highly adaptable, the chipmunk can live in many different habitats. Stays close to burrow and cover such as rock walls, hollow stumps and logs, or rock piles.

Food: Nuts, fruit, seeds, insects, fungi, and small vertebrates. Caches its food in the ground and in its burrow.

Scat: Scat is irregular and indistinguishable from other small rodents.

Chipmunk clues:

Look for neat, round holes in the forest floor, 1 ½ to 2 in. (3.8 to 5.1 cm) in diameter. These holes are the chipmunk's den entrances. Chipmunks go into torpor for winter, waking up to eat from their stored food and then going back into sleep. Listen for the characteristic "chip," trills, or "chuck" sounds.

Breeding: Chipmunks are ready to breed in late February and early March, when they come out on warm days. May have second breeding season in June or July.

Jump:

front rear

WOODCHUCK, *Marmota monax*

Overall Track

- Woodchuck tracks are often curved inward.

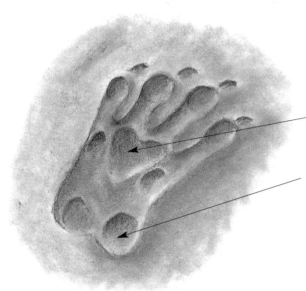

Front Track

4 toes on the front with heavy nails. A vestigial thumb may show in the track.

Plantar and heel pads often show, and the plantar pad often makes a heart-shaped compression.

The heel pads are very prominent on the front track.

Size: 1 ⅞ to 2 ¾ in. (4.8 to 7 cm) long; 1 to 2 in. (2.5 to 5.1 cm) wide

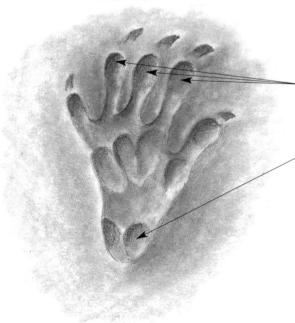

Rear Track

5 toes on the rear with heavy nails.

The three middle toes are often closer together and longer than the others.

Heel pads often do not show as prominently as on the front track.

Size: 1 ⅞ to 2 ¾ in. (4.8 to 7 cm) long; 1 ⅜ to 2 in. (3.5 to 5.1 cm) wide

Trail width (walking): 3 ¼ to 5 ½ in. (8.3 to 14 cm)

Habitat: Stream banks, raised areas, agricultural areas, hedgerows, along highways, or forested areas.

Food: Grasses, other green plants, and especially garden vegetables.

Scat: Scat are rarely found, woodchucks use underground chambers in their burrows as latrines.

Woodchuck clues:
Main entrances to woodchuck burrows will have dirt mounds in front. Woodchucks can climb trees. They hibernate during winter, but tracks can be found in late spring snows, or along stream areas in mud the rest of the year. They leave a 45-degree cut on vegetation, like other rodents.

Breeding: March and April.

Jump:

Walk:

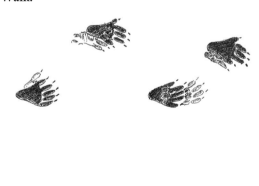

GRAY SQUIRREL, *Sciurus carolinensis*

Overall Track

- Like red squirrels, gray squirrels jump as their common gait pattern, with the front feet either next to or at a slight angle to, each other.
- Gray squirrels' front and rear feet have no fur on them, so often you can see the pads clearly.

Rear Tracks (Top)

5 toes on the rear.

Size: 1 to 1 ¾ in. (2.5 to 4.4 cm) wide

Toes have bulbs on the tips.

The three middle toes are often closer together and longer than the others.

2 heel pads may also show.

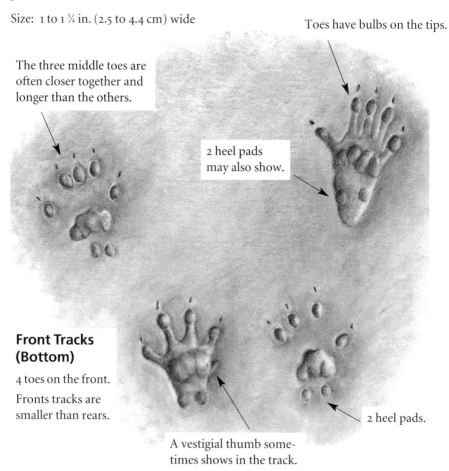

Front Tracks (Bottom)

4 toes on the front.
Fronts tracks are smaller than rears.

2 heel pads.

A vestigial thumb sometimes shows in the track.

Comparisons: Similar to red squirrel, chipmunk, and flying squirrels (page 111); hares and rabbits (page 112).

Trail width: 3 ½ to 6 in. (8.9 to 15.2 cm)

Habitat: Deciduous forests, especially where there is an abundance of nut-bearing trees. Also in parks, suburbs.

Food: Nuts, seeds, fruits and berries, fungi, inner bark of maples and elms, occasionally insects or young birds. Will chew bones, antlers, and turtle shells.

Scat: Scat are variable, small, oval. Can often be found on stumps or downed trees where squirrel has been feeding regularly.

Gray squirrel clues:

Look for large leaf nests in deciduous trees and dens in cavity trees. Look also for holes in snow or ground where the squirrel buried or unearthed stored nuts, broken nut shells, very sharp 45-degree cuts on nipped off twigs lying on the ground at the base of trees (especially oak twigs with acorn caps). Stores nuts often in single nut caches.

Breeding: January and February, and again in late May through early July.

Jump:

front rear

RED SQUIRREL, *Tamiasciurus hudsonicus*

Overall Track

- Red squirrels, like gray squirrels, do a jump as their common gait pattern, and this is a distinguishing feature of their tracks.
- They have furry rear feet with no heel pads.

Rear Tracks (Top)

5 toes on the rear, and in very clear tracks you can see plantar pads.

Size: ⅞ to 1 ⅛ in. (2.2 to 2.9 cm.) wide

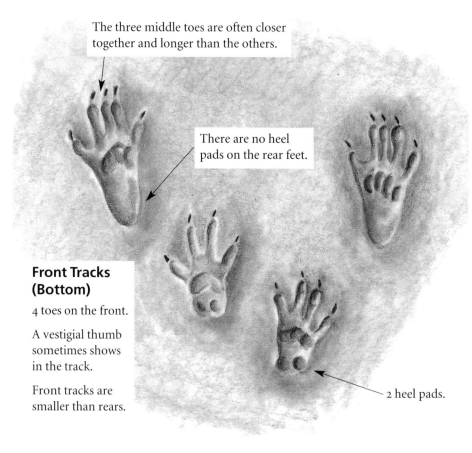

The three middle toes are often closer together and longer than the others.

There are no heel pads on the rear feet.

Front Tracks (Bottom)

4 toes on the front.

A vestigial thumb sometimes shows in the track.

Front tracks are smaller than rears.

2 heel pads.

Comparison: Similar to gray squirrel, flying squirrels, and chipmunk (page 111); hares and rabbits (page 112).

Trail width: 3 to 4 ¼ in. (7.6 to 10.8 cm)

Habitat: Prefers coniferous forests but will occupy mixed or hardwood forests as well.

Food: Acorns, hickory nuts, beechnuts, hemlock cones, tulip and sycamore seeds, sumac fruit, fungi, eggs, insects, nestlings, terminal buds of conifers. Also bark, berries, and buds of maple and elm.

Scat: Scat are small, cylindrical pellets, deposited randomly.

Red squirrel clues:

Look for conifer cones that are stripped down to the shaft, 45-degree cuts on nip twigs of conifers under the trees, middens (piles) of conifer cones and scales from the squirrel eating in one place, and tunnels under the snow. May build a compact twig and leaf nest in trees or nest in cavity tree. Stores food, especially conifer cones, in caches. In winter the trails of red squirrels can easily be found in conifer and mixed deciduous/coniferous forests as they go back and forth over the same path.

Breeding: Late winter to early spring. Will have second mating period in warmer parts of the region from June through July.

Jump:

front rear

FLYING SQUIRREL, NORTHERN, *Glaucomys sabrinus,* and SOUTHERN, *Glaucomys volans*

Overall Track

- Northern flying squirrels are larger than Southern flying squirrels.
- Front tracks fall ahead of the rears more often than happens with other squirrels.

Northern Flying Squirrel

Southern Flying Squirrel

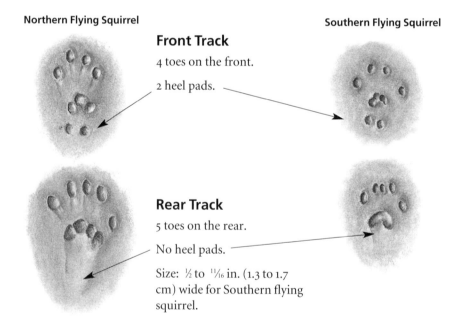

Front Track

4 toes on the front.

2 heel pads.

Rear Track

5 toes on the rear.

No heel pads.

Size: ½ to ¹¹⁄₁₆ in. (1.3 to 1.7 cm) wide for Southern flying squirrel.

Comparisons: Northern flying squirrel trail width is similar to red and gray squirrel. The Southern flying squirrel trail width is similar to chipmunk (page 111).

Trail width: Northern, 3 to 4 in. (7.6 to 10.2 cm); Southern, 1 ½ to 2 ⅞ in. (3.8 to 7.3 cm)

Habitat: Northern flyers prefer old-growth forests. Southern flyers, which are more widespread, can live in a variety of forests habitats.

Food: Northern flyers eat lichen and subterranean fungi as well as pollen, seeds, buds, fruits, above-ground fungi, insects, animal material, fern spores, and tree sap. Southern flyers are nut and seed eaters but will also eat berries, fungi, bark, green buds, and insects. Hickory nuts and white oak acorns are favorites.

Scat: Scat are small pellets that can be found in quantity at the bases of trees that have communal nest cavities.

Flying squirrel clues:

Flying squirrels have flaps of skin between their front and rear legs with which they glide through the air, and in deep snow look for flap drag between the tracks (red squirrels can also leave what look like flap drag but is actually foot drag). Look for flying squirrel nest holes in dead trees with scat piles underneath. Also, when eating nuts, flyers make a smoothly edged, round opening. Both species will nest in groups in winter to conserve heat.

Breeding: Late March to September, with only one litter per year for the Northern species.

Landing from tree, Bound/jump in snow:

Direction of travel

Northern Flying Squirrel

Southern Flying Squirrel

front rear

Flying Squirrel, Northern and Southern | 35

BEAVER, *Castor canadensis*

Overall Track
- Small front foot compared to rear.
- Often there is tail drag or branch drag through the trail that may nearly obliterate the tracks.
- Usually a pigeon-toed walk.

Front Track
Often only 4 toes show.
Front foot is not webbed.

Size: 2 ⅞ to 3 ⅞ in. (7.3 to 9.8 cm) long
2 ¾ to 3 ½ in. (7 to 8.9 cm) wide

A fifth toe may show in a very clear track.

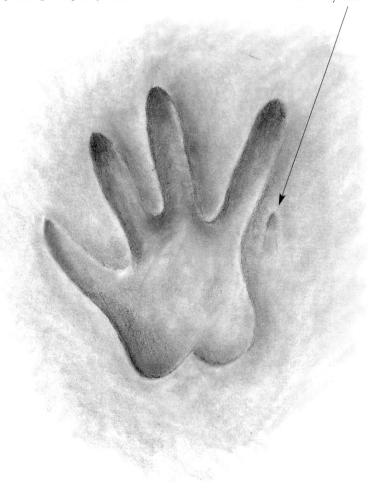

Rear Track

5 toes on the rear, and the rear is significantly larger than front.

Size: 5 to 7 in. (12.7 to 17.8 cm) long; 3 ¼ to 5 ¼ in. (8.3 to 13.3 cm) wide

Rear track often shows webbing.

Broad, heavy nails.

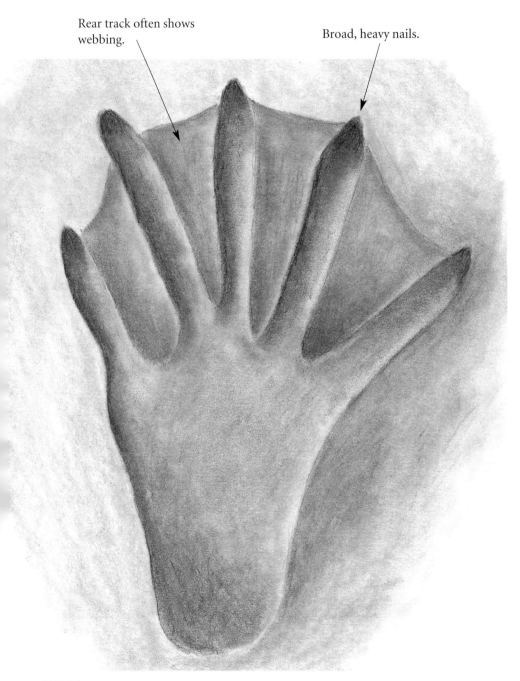

front rear

Beaver cut trees:

Lodge and dam:

Trail width: 6 to 10 ¾ in. (15.2 to 27.3 cm)

Habitat: Wetlands, ponds, slow-moving rivers.

Food: Trees, aquatic succulents, herbaceous plants. Favors aspen but will eat a wide variety of tree species.

Scat: Usually not seen as it is deposited in the water.

Beaver clues:

Beavers build scent mounds of vegetation where they deposit urine and "castoreum," a yellowish substance secreted from the anus. Also look for dams, cut trees debarked close to the base with teethmarks, sticks in waterbodies, lodges, bank dens in rivers, and canals leading from rivers, ponds or wetlands. Beaver cache sticks in front of their lodges as winter food.

Breeding: January into March.

Walk:

front rear

DEER MOUSE, *Peromyscus maniculatus,* and WHITE-FOOTED MOUSE,
Peromyscus leucopus

Front Track

4 toes on front.

2 heel pads.

Size: ¼ to ½ in. (.64 to 1.3 cm) long; ⅜ to ½ in. (.38 to 1.3 cm) wide

Rear Track

5 toes on rear.

The three middle toes are often closer together and longer than the other two toes.

Has 3 heel pads, but these rarely all show.

Size: ¼ to ½ in. (.64 to 1.3 cm) long; ⅜ to ½ in. (.38 to 1.3 cm) wide.

Full jumping pattern
Lower tracks are the fronts, upper tracks are the rears.

Comparison: Similar to vole and shrew (page 109); chipmunk (page 111); jumping mouse (page 113).

Mice clues:

Look for middens of food debris, especially in openings at the bases of trees, under ledges, and in open spaces under boulders and in hollow logs. Also look for caches of food and nests of finely shredded leaves, bark, grasses, and other fibers. In the forest, cherry pits with small holes in them are signs of mice activity.

Trail width: 1 ⅜ to 1 ¼ in. (3.5 to 4.4 cm)

Habitat: Deer mice and white-footed mice are very similar and both inhabit most terrestrial habitats in the Northeastern United States.

Food: Mice are omnivorous and will eat seeds, nutlets, fungi, berries, and insects.

Scat: Mice deposit small pellets randomly.

Breeding: Early March through late October.

Jump:

Tail drag

White-Footed Mouse

Deer Mouse

front rear

VOLES, *Microtus* and *Clethrionomys*

Front Track

4 toes.

Rear Track

5 toes.

Scat: Voles make latrines in their runs where they deposit small cylindrical pellets.

Comparison: Similar to mice and shrew (page 109).

Trail width in snow:
1 in. or more (2.5 cm)

Meadow Vole, *Microtus pennsylvanicus*

Trail Width: 1 ⅝ in. (4.1 cm)*

Habitat: Open areas, including fields, orchards, pastures, meadows, saltwater marshes, borders of water bodies, open woods, and clear-cuts.

Food: Eats mostly vegetation.

Vole clues:

Voles usually walk and shuffle but they can also jump. Will make runways in snow or tall grasses. Meadow voles leave chewed-off pieces of grasses in their runs. Look for small green scat in meadow runways.

Woodland or Pine Vole, *Microtus pinetorum*

Trail width: Unknown. Lives mostly underground.

Habitat: Found in a wide variety of habitats.

Food: Roots, bark, tubers, stems of grasses, fungi, berries, seeds, nuts. Forages mostly below ground.

Southern Red-Backed Vole, *Clethrionomys gapperi*

Trail width: 1 ¼ in. (3.2 cm)*

Habitat: Moist deciduous, coniferous, and mixed woodlands, with cover. Can be found in clearcuts, talus slopes, and stone walls.

Food: Vegetation, berries, fruits, nuts, fungi, seeds, tree roots, bark, and insects.

Rock Vole, *Microtus chrotorrhinus*

Trail width: 1 in. (2.5 cm)*

Habitat: Forests of higher elevations. Talus slopes, moss covered boulders, near stream areas.

Food: Mosses, bunchberry, larvae, fungi, insects.

*Note: Trail width for voles marked with asterisk are based on study skin measurements.

MUSKRAT, *Ondatra zibethicus*

Overall Track

- Look for front and rear tracks that are of significantly different sizes.
- Muskrats have stiff hairs along the edges of all their toes that may show in the tracks.
- Tail drag often shows as well; the tail will appear as a line through the track.

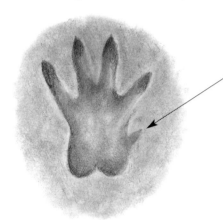

Front Track

4 toes on the front.

A vestigial toe on the front sometimes shows as a slight impression or as a nail mark.

Size: 1 ⅛ to 1 ½ in. (2.9 to 3.8 cm) long; 1 ⅛ to 1 ½ in. (2.9 to 3.8 cm) wide

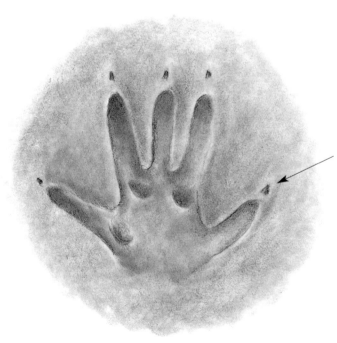

Rear Track

5 toes on the rear.

The lowest toe is to the inside.

Size: 1 ⅝ to 2 ¾ in. (4.1 to 6.9 cm) long; 1 ½ to 2 ⅛ in. (3.8 to 5.4 cm) wide

Muskrat clues:

Muskrat tracks are found near water. Look for bank burrows in rivers and streams, with entrances just below the surface of the water (sometimes with sticks in them). In ponds look for lodges made of mud, plants, and small sticks (beavers make their lodges of larger sticks and branches), feeding platforms on the water, and canals in marshes. In winter muskrats make enclosed pushups of mud and plants out over the ice that serve to keep breathing holes open in the ice, and that are used also as feeding stations inside. Also look for cut vegetation near water or floating in water.

Trail width: 3 ¼ to 5 in. (8.3 to 12.7 cm)

Habitat: Shallow wetlands that support varied aquatic plants, streams, and wooded swamps. Most abundant in areas of cattails.

Food: Roots and stalks of cattails, grasses, also some freshwater clams, fish, and crustaceans.

Scat: Muskrats will often deposit scat on floating logs, and rocks that are protruding above water. Scat pellets have a melted look and can be stuck together in masses.

Breeding: Late February through fall. Prolific breeders.

Walk, with tail drag:

front rear

NORWAY RAT, *Rattus norvegicus*

Overall Track

- The outer toes often point in opposite directions on both front and rear tracks.

Front Track

4 toes on front.

Size: ¾ to ⅞ in. (1.9 to 2.2 cm) long; ½ to 1 in. (1.3 to 2.5 cm)* wide

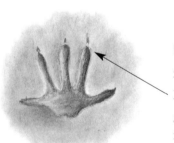

Rear Track

5 toes on the rear.

Middle toes often parallel.

Size: 1 to 1¼ in. (2.5 to 3.2 cm) long; ⅞ to 1 in. (2.2 to 2.5 cm) wide*

Norway rat clues:

Norway rat tracks are easy to find in urban areas and in developed areas near water sources.

Habitat: Near human activity, either agricultural or in suburban or urban environments. Waste dumps and waterfront areas. Also abundant in the salt marshes of the coast.

Food: Norway rats will try to eat almost anything.

Scat: Long, cylindrical pellets.

Breeding: Prolific.

Walk:

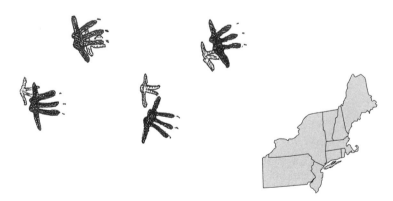

*Note: These measurements are based on my own and those from Olaus Murie.

MEADOW JUMPING MOUSE, *Zapus hudsonicus,* and WOODLAND JUMPING MOUSE, *Napaeozapus insignis*

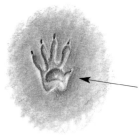

Front Track

4 toes on the front.

A vestigial thumb may show.

Size: Approximately ½ in. (1.3 cm) long

Rear Track

5 toes on the rear.

Very long heel.

Size: Approximately 1 in. (2.5 cm) long

Comparisons: Jumping mice are similar to other mice (page 113).

Trail width: 1 ⅝ to 2 in. (4.1 to 5.1 cm)

Habitat: Meadow jumping mice live in many habitats, including grassy fields, thickets along streams, edges of ponds or woodlands, and swamps. They need moist, loose soils to burrow in. Woodland jumping mice prefer moist woods with herbaceous low cover. May prefer hardwoods to softwoods.

Food: Jumping mice are omnivorous and will eat seeds, nuts, fungi, berries, rootlets, and insects.

Scat: Mice deposit small pellets randomly.

> **Jumping mice clues:**
>
> Jumping mice have a profound hibernation season and are not seen from October or November until April or May.

Breeding: May to August.

Jump:

Meadow Jumping Mouse

Woodland Jumping Mouse

front rear

PORCUPINE, *Erethizon dorsatum*

Overall Track

- Porcupines have very nubbly foot pads with no fur on them.
- Often toes don't show, only the full foot pad and nails.

Front Track

4 toes on the front.

Nails far ahead of the toes.

Size: 2 ¼ to 3 ⅜ in. (5.7 to 8.6 cm) long; 1 ¼ to 1 ⅞ in. (3.2 to 4.8 cm) wide

Rear Track

5 toes on the rear.

Nails closer to the toes.

Size: 2 ¾ to 3 ⅞ in. (7 to 9.9 cm) long; 1 ½ to 2 in. (3.8 to 5.1 cm) wide

Trail width: 5 to 9 in. (12.7 to 22.9 cm)

Habitat: Needs extensive stands of spruce, pine, hemlock, and deciduous/coniferous mixed forests, with available denning sites.

Food: Vegetarian. Warm-weather foods include sugar maple buds, leaves of young beech trees, oak, basswood and ash leaves, forbes, aspens, raspberry leaves, apples (leaves and fruit), acorns, and beechnuts. Winter foods include hemlock needles and small branches and the inner bark of spruce, white pine, elm, basswood, beech, and sugar maple. Porcupines need salt to balance the potassium from their regular foods and will chew on anything that will offer them sodium, including things touched by sweaty human hands, signs, areas with road salt, and certain plants like waterlilies.

> **Porcupine clues:**
>
> Look for bark chewed off of trees in large patches with teeth marks, nip twigs with rough, 45-degree cuts, oak twigs with rough, 45-degree cuts and acorn caps left on, quills on the ground, and dens in boulder mounds and ledges as well as in logs and hollow trees. Troughs in the snow with a taildrag obscuring the tracks are typical of porcupine.

Scat and urine: Scat are variable but most often long pellets of coarse fiber. Porcupine scat and urine in winter smell piney. Scat can accumulate at the base of trees or at the entrance of dens, or in regularly used trails.

Breeding: In autumn.

Walk:

DOMESTIC DOG, *Canis familiaris*

Overall Track

- The domestic dog has been bred for so many functions that size is highly variable.
- Most dog tracks, however, will show more splay than their wild relatives, and usually their trail will wander all over, whereas their wild relatives will go in a straight line.
- Like other canids:
  - The track is an oval compression shape with symmetrical positioning of toes.
  - The track shows a raised mound in the middle between the toes and plantar pad.
  - The rear foot is smaller than the front foot.
  - The plantar pad is pointed on the leading edge.
  - An X can be drawn through both the front and rear tracks like this:

Front Track

Toes splay out.

Front track is larger than rear track.

Plantar pad is pointed with a single lobe.

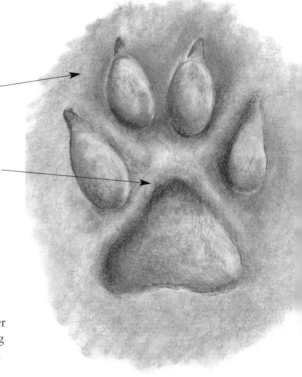

Comparisons: Larger dogs may have tracks similar to coyote and wolf (page 114); mountain lion (page 115); river otter (page 117). Domestic dog puppy tracks can be mistaken for bobcat tracks, as they are rounder than adult dogs.

Dog clues:

Dog trails wander a great deal and look sloppy in comparison to their wild cousins. Wild canids have a very narrow trail width in comparison to most dogs and go in a straight line through the woods, unless they are engaged in hunting, mating, or play.

Rear Track

Toes may not be as spread out as on the front foot.

Rear track is smaller than the front track.

Scat and urine: Dog scat is often distinguishable from other canid scat by its grainy texture (from eating grain-based dry dog food). Wild canid scat is primarily composed of meat, bone, hair, and wild fruits or plants. If dogs are feeding on wild game, however, their scat will look like fox, coyote, or wolf. Dogs use urine to scent mark.

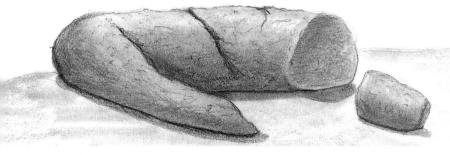

Track patterns: See gray wolf.

front rear

GRAY WOLF, *Canis lupus*

Overall Track

- Largest track of the wild canid family and larger than most domestic dogs.
- Like other canids:
  - The track is an oval compression shape with symmetrical positioning of toes.
  - The track shows a raised mound in the middle between the toes and plantar pad.
  - The rear foot is smaller than the front foot.
  - The plantar pad is pointed on the leading edge.
  - An X can be drawn through both the front and rear tracks like this:

Front track

Front track inner toes are not usually as splayed as a domestic dog's tracks.

Size: 3 ⅞ to 5 ½ in. (9.8 to 14 cm) long; 2 ¼ to 4 ¼ in. (5.7 to 10.3 cm) wide

Comparisons: Similar to large domestic dog and coyote (page 114).

Rear Track

Size: 3 ⅛ to 4 ¾ in. (7.9 to 12 cm) long;
2 ⅜ to 2 ¾ in. (6 to 7 cm) wide

front rear

Trail width: 3 to 7 in. (7.6 to 17.8 cm)

Habitat: Open to wooded habitat.

Food: Primarily medium to large mammals. Deer, moose, and beaver are favored.

Scat and urine: Scat is most often found in the middle of trails, at the junctures of trails, and on raised objects such as stumps or stones. Wolf and coyote scat overlap in size. Wolves, like other canids, use scat and urine to scent mark their territories. Scat has a very strong odor. Shown here at half size.

Wolf clues:

Look for scent posts, dens. Listen for the characteristic long how of the wolf as opposed to the short howl and yipping of the coyote.

Breeding: Mid- winter to early spring.

Return of the wolf to the northeast: A wolf killed in Maine in 1993, along with credible wolf sightings in parts of Northern Maine, may or may not mean that wolves are moving back to New England and re-establishing a viable population. Wolves can now be found in Quebec only twenty miles from the U.S. border, across the St. Lawrence River.

In 1998, researchers Daniel Harrison and Theodore Chapin studied the extent, distribution, and connectivity of potential habitat for wolves in the northeastern United States.[1] They found that there are two potential corridors where wolves may cross the St. Lawrence river into Maine. If they can cross the river, there is sufficient potential habitat in northern, western, and eastern Maine and in northern New Hampshire and Vermont to support a healthy wolf population. New York state may also have adequate habitat, but currently there appears to be geographic barriers to natural dispersal to that area.

In addition to the question of the wolf's ability to disperse across the border, there remains the question of whether human attitudes will support their return.

Wolf, Dog, and Coyote Track Patterns

The larger canids can sometimes direct-register walk or trot, though it is less common than in the foxes or cats. They more often walk with rears falling ahead of or behind the fronts. They will also sometimes pace.

Walks and trots:

Oblique trot (rear off to one side of body):

Lope:

Gallop:

front rear

COYOTE, *Canis latrans*

Overall Track

- Like other canids:
  - The track is an oval compression shape with symmetrical positioning of toes.
  - The track shows a raised mound in the middle between the toes and plantar.
  - The rear foot is smaller than the front foot.
  - The plantar pad is pointed on the leading edge.
  - An X can be drawn through both the front and rear tracks like this:

Front Track

Inner nails are close together and point forward.

Toes are tight together, with outer toes close in behind inner toes. Quite often the nails on the outer toes don't show.

Plantar pad is pointed, with a single lobe.

Size: 2 ⅞ to 3 ½ in. (7.3 to 8.9 cm) long; 1 ⅞ to 2 ½ in. (4.8 to 6.4 cm) wide

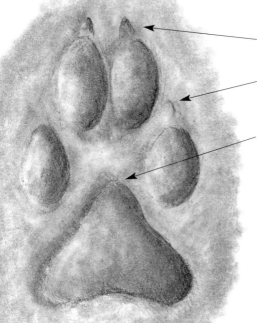

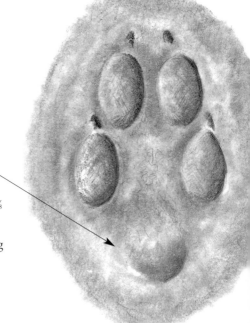

Rear Track

Rear track often shows only a small compression for plantar pad.

Size: 2 ½ to 3 in. (6.4 to 7.6 cm) long; 1 ⅝ to 2 ⅛ in. (4.1 to 5.4 cm) wide

Comparisons: Similar to domestic dog or wolf (page 114); red fox (page 116).

Trail width: 2 ½ to 5 ½ in. (6.4 to 14 cm) when trotting, wider when walking.

Habitat: Very adaptable to diverse habitats. Not often found in dense forests.

Food: Rodents, hares and rabbits, ground birds, snakes, insects, fruit, berries, plants, carrion.

Scat and urine: Scat is most often found in the middle of trails, at the junctures of trails, and on raised objects such as stumps or stones. Coyote and fox scat may overlap in size. Coyotes use scat and urine to scent mark their territories.

Coyote clues:

Look for a straight, tight trail. Coyotes like to utilize human-created trails and back roads. Deer kills will be eaten from the rear by coyotes. Dens in banks, rock outcrops, gullies, or overhangs. Coyotes are social animals and will be found in packs as well as in pairs or alone. Listen for the characteristic yipping and howling song of the coyote.

Track patterns: See gray wolf.

front rear

RED FOX, *Vulpes vulpes*

Overall Track

- The red fox track is shaped like an arrowhead.
- Due to the hairiness of the red fox's foot, the track often doesn't show clear toe pads but is instead fuzzy. In mud or wet sand, the fur can be seen in the tracks.
- Like other canids:
  - The track is an oval compression shape with symmetrical positioning of toes.
  - The track shows a raised mound in the middle between the toes and plantar pad.
  - The rear foot is smaller than the front foot.
  - The plantar pad is pointed on the leading edge.
  - An X can be drawn through both the front and rear tracks like this:

Front Track

The distinguishing feature of the red fox track is a bar or chevron in the heel pad of the front foot.

Often, however, the rear track is superimposed on the front and the bar or chevron may not show.

Size: 2 ⅛ to 2 ⅞ in. (5.4 to 7.3 cm) long; 1 ⅝ to 2 ⅛ in. (4.1 to 5.4 cm) wide

Comparisons: Similar to coyote (page 116); gray fox (page 118).

Red fox pouncing on vole under the snow

Rear Track

Size: 1 ¾ to 2 ½ in. (4.4 to 6.4 cm) long; 1 ½ to 1 ⅞ in. (3.9 to 4.8 cm) wide

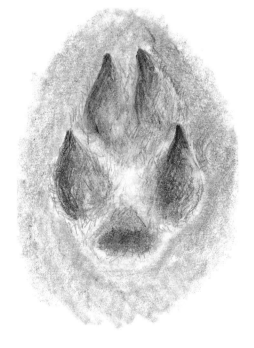

front rear

Red fox clues:

Look for ground dens with loose dirt in front of them, along with feathers, bones, hair, and scat around the entrance. Foxes will also den in rock crevices and boulder mounds. Scent posts are easy to find on fox trails in winter, as the skunky smell of the urine is strongest in January and February. The trail of the red fox is usually very narrow and straight. Will cache food. Red fox will walk on stone walls and on fallen logs.

Trail width: 2 to 3 ⅞ in. (5.1 to 9.8 cm) when trotting, wider when walking.

Habitat: Can occupy a diverse range of habitats. Favors fields mixed with woods, marshes, and streams. Likes forest edges and openings in heavily forested areas. Can be found in suburban and urban areas as well.

Food: Omnivorous. Winter foods usually consist of mice and rats, rabbits, birds, carrion, apples, and dried berries. Spring, summer, and fall foods consist of rabbits, rodents, small mammals, birds, snakes, turtles and eggs, grasshoppers and other insects, fawns, berries, grasses, nuts, fruits, and grains.

Scat and urine: Red fox scat is long and tapered and is used for marking. Scat is most often found in the middle of trails, at the junctures of trails, and on raised objects such as stumps or stones. Fox scat in winter can be distinguished from other animals, but it is harder to distinguish other times of year as it can look very much like other animals who eat similar foods. In winter, it is made up of hair, usually from small rodents. Scat that are ½ in. (1.3 cm) or under in diameter, deposited on trails or raised objects, full of rodent hair, and not tightly twisted can be considered red or gray fox. Urine has a very strong skunky odor and is used for marking.

Breeding: January and February.

Red and Gray Fox Track Patterns

Foxes will commonly direct-register walk and trot, though they will also walk with rears falling ahead or behind the fronts, or trot with rears falling ahead of the fronts.

Walk:

A direct-register trot will have a very narrow trail width.

Oblique trot (rear off to one side of body):

Lope:

Gallop:

front rear

GRAY FOX, *Urocyon cinereoargenteus*

Overall Track

- Gray fox tracks exhibit characteristics of both the dog and cat families. The compression shape is relatively round, like the cats, and may or may not show nails, as the gray fox has semiretractible nails.
- The track is symmetrical and has a somewhat pointed plantar pad like those of other canids, but the negative space between toes and plantar pad is greater than on other canids.
- Gray fox will direct register when trotting (like red fox and cats).
- Like other canids:
  - The track shows a raised mound in the middle between the toes and plantar pad.
  - The rear foot is smaller than the front foot.
  - An X can be drawn though both front and rear tracks like this:

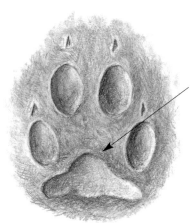

Front Track

Plantar pad is uniquely shaped, being shallower lengthwise than on other canid front tracks.

Size: 1 ⅜ to 2 in. (3.5 to 5.1 cm) long; 1 ¼ to 1 ⅞ in. (3.2 to 4.8 cm) wide

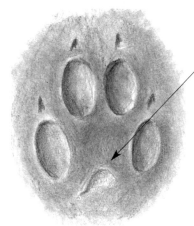

Rear Track

Very small plantar pad compression in track.

Size: 1 ¼ to 1 ¾ in. (3.2 to 4.4 cm) long; 1 to 1 ¾ in. (2.5 to 4.4 cm) wide

Comparisons: Similar to red fox (page 118); housecat (page 119).

Gray fox clues:

Look for a trail pattern similar to a cat's. The gray fox usually has a wider trail width than red fox. Don't assume that a trail going up a tree is a cat. It could be the gray fox!

Trail width: 1 ¾ to 4 in. (4.4 to 10.2 cm)

Habitat: Typically lives in deciduous forests in the Eastern United States, but may be found in a variety of habitats.

Food: Cottontail rabbits, small mammals, birds, reptiles, insects, fruit, nuts, grasses, and carrion.

Scat and urine: Gray fox will scent mark with urine that smells mildly skunk-like but not as strong as that of the red fox. Scat is similar to the red fox, long and tapered and placed at trail junctures, on rocks and stumps, and at high spots on trails as markers.

Breeding: January though April.

Track patterns: See red fox.

front   rear

BLACK BEAR, *Ursus americana*

Overall Track
- Very humanlike print, with 5 toes on front and back.
- Toe sizes are reversed from that of a human track, with the smallest toe on the inside and the largest on the outside.

Front Track

Nails are long and extend far ahead of toes.

Innermost toe is smaller than the others, and sometimes doesn't show in track.

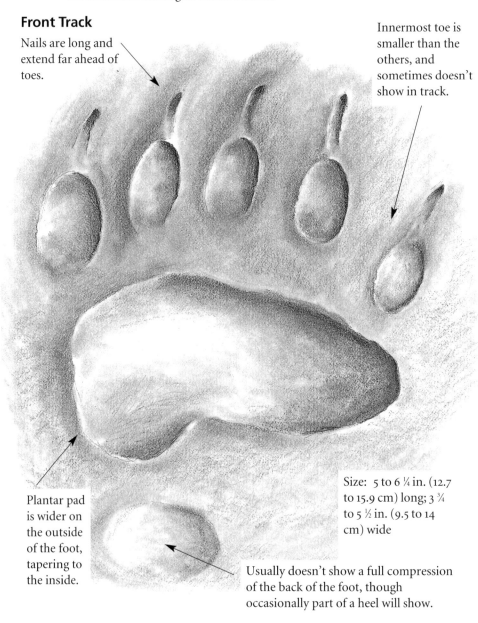

Plantar pad is wider on the outside of the foot, tapering to the inside.

Size: 5 to 6 ¼ in. (12.7 to 15.9 cm) long; 3 ¾ to 5 ½ in. (9.5 to 14 cm) wide

Usually doesn't show a full compression of the back of the foot, though occasionally part of a heel will show.

Rear Track

The whole impression of the foot often appears on the rear track.

Nails are closer to the toes than on the front.

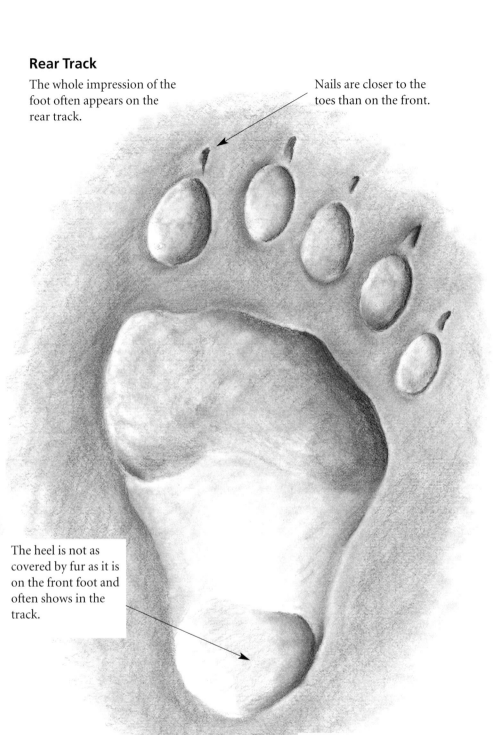

The heel is not as covered by fur as it is on the front foot and often shows in the track.

Size: 6 to 7 ¾ in. (15.2 to 19.7 cm) long; 3 ½ to 5 ½ in. (8.9 to 14 cm) wide

front rear

Trail width: 9 ½ to 14 ½ in. (24.1 to 36.8 cm)

Habitat: Prefers wilder areas with thick understory, varied habitat, and lots of mast trees. Forest openings provide berries and ant pupae. Adaptable but needs large territory.

Food: Bears are omnivores that eat wetland plants, grasses, clovers, buds of beech and ironwood, cattails, berries, nuts, carrion, eggs and nestlings, small mammals, bees, larvae, ants and other insects. Bears will eat fawns when they find them, but mammals are a very small percentage of their diet. Though naturally cautious of humans, bears will eat birdseed from feeders and raid garbage cans and campgrounds.

Scat: Scat is variable according to diet but often it is in a loose pile or in sections of variable pieces. Often it is in copious amounts and of even consistency. Shown here at two-thirds size:

Scat composed of vegetation

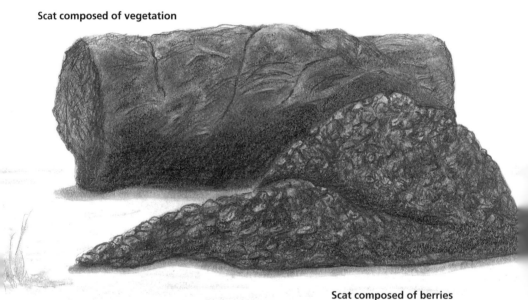

Scat composed of berries

Breeding: Mid-June to mid-July. Delayed implantation means cubs are born in late January.

Walk: **Lope to Gallop:**

Black bear clues:

Look for bitten trees; broken limbs; bear "nests," which are collections of broken limbs that the bear has eaten from and left high in the tree; dug up holes; torn-up, rotting logs; claw marks on trees (especially easy to see on beech); bites on utility poles. Powerline and railroad right of ways are frequented. In spring check wetlands and seeps, where bears eat emerging vegetation. Bears in winter will den up and undergo torpor.

Bear Sign

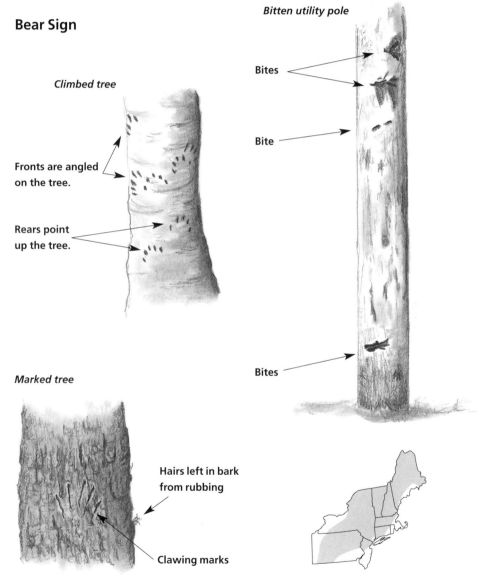

Bitten utility pole

Bites

Bite

Bites

Climbed tree

Fronts are angled on the tree.

Rears point up the tree.

Marked tree

Hairs left in bark from rubbing

Clawing marks

front   rear

RACCOON, *Procyon lotor*

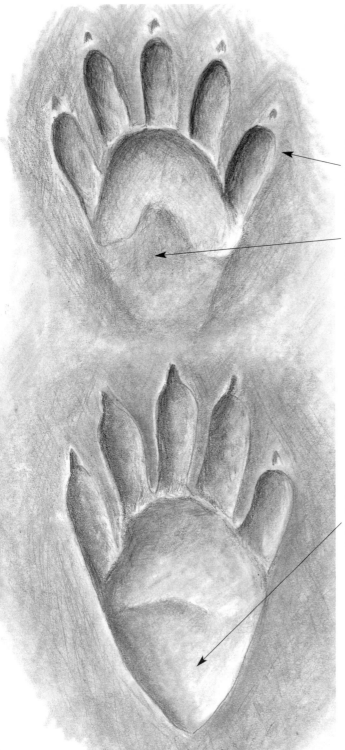

Overall Track

- Long, chubby fingers
- C-shaped plantar pads

Front Track

5 elongated toes. The inner toe is not opposable but is often used like a thumb.

The full heel pad rarely shows on the front track.

Size: 2 to 3 in. (5.1 to 7.6 cm) long; 1 ⅞ to 2 ½ in (4.8 to 6.4 cm) wide

Rear Track

5 elongated toes.

The heel pad is more likely to appear in the rear track.

Size: 2 ⅜ to 3 ¾ in. (6 to 9.4 cm) long; 2 ⅜ to 2 ½ in. (6 to 6.4 cm) wide

Trail width: 3 ¼ to 6 in. (8.3 to 15.2 cm)

Habitat: Woods and wetlands that provide food and den sites, swamps and marshes, upland woods, cultivated areas, suburban and urban areas.

Food: Omnivorous and highly opportunistic.

Scat: Scat is highly variable but usually has blunt ends. Raccoons sometimes make latrines along their walkways and paths. Scat may be deposited on fallen logs, at the bases of trees, on stumps or rocks, on the horizontal limbs of trees, or on stone walls.

> **Raccoon clues:**
>
> Raccoons have very sensitive pads and so they like to walk on smooth or soft surfaces. Look for tracks in mud beside streams as raccoons like to stay close to water where they forage for crustaceans and fish.

Note: It is dangerous to handle or smell raccoon scat, as it may contain a parasitic roundworm whose eggs can be inhaled!

Breeding: January to March.

Walk:

Fast Walk:

front rear

WEASELS, LONG-TAILED, *Mustela frenata*, SHORT-TAILED, *Mustela erminea*, and LEAST, *Mustela nivalis*

Overall Track

- Like other mustelids:
  - Placement of toes is asymmetrical, with the slope going toward the inside of the track. The plantar pad also slopes toward the inside.
  - There is a small heel pad on the front foot only.

Long-tailed Weasel

Trail width: 1 ½ to 3 in. (3.8 to 7.6 cm)

Trail pattern: Frenetic and often inconsistent gait.

Short-tailed Weasel

Train width: 1 to 2 ⅛ in. (2.5 to 5.4 cm)

Trail pattern: Fairly consistent bounding pattern of one short bound, one long bound, with drag connecting the short bounds.

Long-tailed weasel

Short-tailed weasel or Ermine

Least Weasel

Trail width: ⅞ to 1 ⅝ in. (2.2 to 4.1 cm)

Comparisons: The long-tailed weasel's tracks can be similar to mink (page 120).

Habitat: The long-tailed weasel is the most widespread of the weasels. It can be found in a variety of habitats but usually near bodies of water—swamps, wetlands, creeks, etc. The short-tailed weasel lives most often in the coniferous forests of the north, but it can be found in all but the coastal areas of the northeastern United States. It utilizes brushy areas bordering fields, hedgerows, and stone walls. Least weasels dwell in the forests of the high Allegheny mountains of Pennsylvania and into western New York in the Northeast.

> **Weasel clues:**
>
> The best way to distinguish weasels is by trail pattern and width. Least weasels occur in only a small portion of the Northeast, being more abundant farther west. All species of weasels will cache food.

Food: All weasels will eat mice, voles, chipmunks, shrews, frogs, lizards, small snakes, birds, and insects.

Scat: Twisted and often folded back on itself, with smaller hairs than that usually found in larger mustelids.

Breeding: June, and until females are bred. Long-tailed and short-tailed weasels have delayed implantation in which the fertilized egg develops for around two weeks and then goes dormant for 9 to 10 months. It resumes development in the late winter, and young are born mid-April. The least weasel breeds throughout the year but intensifies in spring and late summer. Implantation in the least weasel is not delayed like other mustelids.

Gaits: The long-tailed weasel leaves an erratic trail pattern, and in winter it usually does a bounding gait.

The short-tailed weasel often does two short bounds, followed by a longer one.

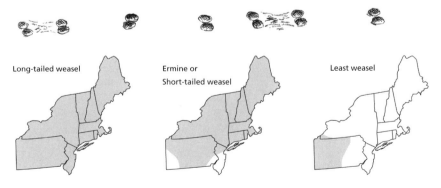

Long-tailed weasel

Ermine or
Short-tailed weasel

Least weasel

front rear

MINK, *Mustela vison*

Overall Track

- Look for the star shape in the front tracks and for the characteristic bounding or loping track patterns characteristic of the larger weasels.
- Like other mustelids:
  - Placement of toes is asymmetrical, with the slope going toward the inside of the track. The plantar pad also slopes toward the inside.
  - There is a small heel pad on the front foot only.

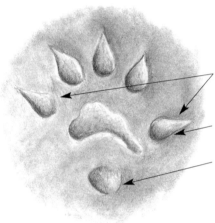

Front Track

Look for a star-shaped pattern. The mink's outer toes on the front track often show nearly opposite each other.

Small inner toe may not show all the time.

The heel pad may or may not show.

Size: 1 ¼ to 2 in. (3.2 to 5.1 cm) long, up to 2 ⅝ in. (6.7 cm) if heel pad shows. 1 ¼ to 1 ¾ in. (3.2 to 4.4 cm) wide

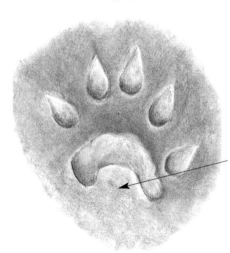

Rear Track

The heel area of the foot often doesn't show, but when it does, it can add length to the track.

No heel pad.

Size: 1 ¼ to 1 ⅞ in. (3.2 to 4.8 cm) long, up to 2 ⅞ in. (7.3 cm) if heel area shows. 1 ⅛ in. to 1 ¾ in. (2.9 to 4.4 cm) wide

Comparisons: Similar to long-tailed weasel (page 120); marten (page 121).

Trail width: 2 ½ to 4 in. (6.4 to 10.2 cm)

Habitat: Various wetland habitats, including cattail marshes, small streams, rivers, swamps, beaver ponds, lakes, tidal flats.

Food: Crayfish, fish, frogs, small mammals including muskrat, birds, snakes, and invertebrates.

Scat: Scat is usually twisted and folded back on itself.

Mink clues:

Look for mink tracks around streams, rivers, and wetlands. Sometimes uses old beaver lodges or muskrat bank burrows for den sites. The mink occasionally makes "slides" that are three to four inches but sometimes up to five inches (7.6 to 12.7 cm) wide in snow. Slides are formed when the animal goes sledding on its belly, sometimes pushing with its feet. It slides into water, on level ground, or downhill. Caches food.

Look for mink scat on rocks, stumps, and hummocks. Like other mustelids, mink like to mark with scat on prominent parts of their landscape.

Breeding: January through early April. As with most mustelids, the mink has a delayed implantation. For mink this delay can last up to 6 weeks.

Gaits: See marten. When the mink bounds, it does so with a more consistent stride length than the long-tailed weasel.

front rear

MARTEN, *Martes americana*

Overall Track
- The marten's feet are heavily furred, and the pads are not well developed.
- Nails on marten are semiretractable, so they may or may not show clearly.
- Like other mustelids:
  - Placement of toes is asymmetrical, with the slope going toward the inside of the track. The plantar pad also slopes toward the inside.
  - There is a small heel pad on the front foot only.

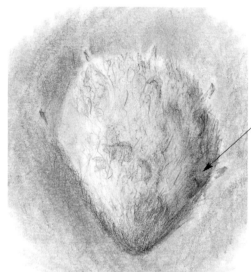

WINTER TRACKS:
Front Track
If pads show at all, they tend to show toward one side of the foot.

Inner toe impressions rarely show.

Size: 1 ⅝ to 2 ⅝ in. (4.1 to 6.7 cm) long; 1 ½ to 2 ⅝ in. (3.8 to 6.7 cm) wide

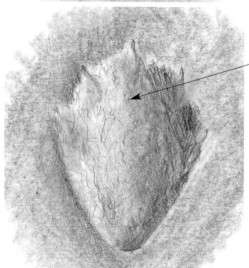

Rear Track
Plantar pads are even less developed on the rear and rarely show.

Size: 1 ⅝ to 2 ⅝ in. (4.1 to 6.7 cm) long; 1 ½ to 2 ⅝ in. (3.8 to 6.7 cm) wide

Comparisons: Similar to mink (page 121); fisher (page 122).

SUMMER TRACKS:

In summer the marten's feet lose some fur and the pads may show more clearly.

Front Track

Rear Track

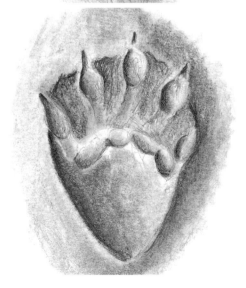

front rear

> **Marten clues:**
>
> Like its cousin the fisher, the marten will cross and recross its paths,
> checking stumps, holes, and trees. Highly energetic animal. Will scent mark
> on branches and logs by rubbing its abdominal scent glands along them.
> Dens in hollow trees. To distinguish marten tracks from fisher tracks, look
> for the inner toe. In a study done in 1995, researchers found that 80 percent
> of all tracks from martens were missing the impression of the inner toe,
> whereas this was not the case with the fisher.[2]

Trail width: 2 ⅞ to 4 ¼ in. (7.3 to 10.8 cm)

Habitat: Mature of old-growth northern spruce and balsam fir forests, or mixed
coniferous/deciduous forests.
Martens need a complex forest floor structure that includes dead trunks,
branches, and plenty of litter. Martens avoid early to mid-successional forests,
and forest openings.

Food: Primary foods are red squirrels and voles. Will also eat fruit, mice, shrews,
birds, snowshoe hare, and carrion.

Scat: Scat is long, thin, and often twisted, with small bones and hair.
Occasionally contains fruit, which distinguishes it from the scat of the smaller
weasels and mink, but not from fisher. Deposited on prominent objects and on
trails.

Breeding: Late July or August. As with most mustelids, the marten breeds
shortly after giving birth, as it has a delayed implantation that can last 10–11
months.

Gaits of the larger Mustelids (Mink, Fisher, Marten and Otter):

Bounding:

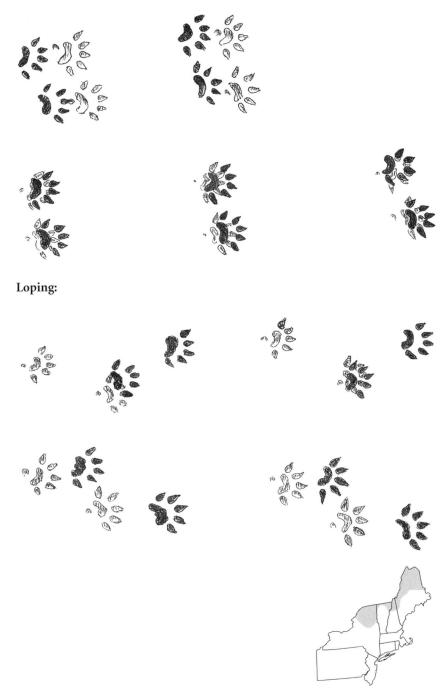

Loping:

front rear

FISHER, *Martes pennanti*

Overall Track

- Toes appear somewhat rounded or oval.
- Nails on fishers are semiretractable, so they may or may not show clearly.
- Like other mustelids:
  - Placement of toes is asymmetrical, with the slope going toward the inside of the track. The plantar pad also slopes toward the inside.
  - There is a small heel pad on the front foot only.

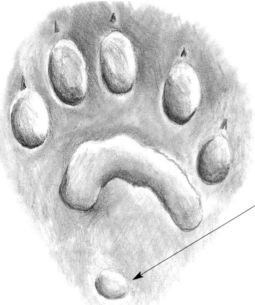

Front Track

When the heel pad shows in the track it makes the front foot appear much larger than the rear.

Size: 2 ⅛ to 2 ⅞ in. (5.4 to 9.8 cm) long and up to 5 in. (12.7 cm) when heel pad appears; 2 ⅛ to 4 in. (5.4 to 10.2 cm) wide

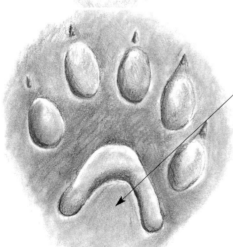

Rear Track

No heel pad on rear track, though a compression of the heel area may show.

Size: 2 ⅛ to 3 in. (5.4 to 7.6 cm) long; 2 to 3 in. (5.1 to 7.6 cm) wide

Comparisons: Similar to river otter (page 123); marten (page 122). When the inner toe doesn't show, fisher tracks can look like bobcat (page 125).

Trail width: 3 to 5 ½ in. (7.6 to 14 cm)

Habitat: Coniferous and mixed coniferous/hardwood forests. Also does well in areas of extensive second-growth woodlands.

Food: Snowshoe hare, porcupine, carrion of deer, other small and medium-sized mammals and birds. Will also eat fruit, berries, and nuts.

Scat and urine: Scat is twisted, narrow, tight, and often folded back on itself. Scat is often composed of hair or fur. Fishers deposit scat and urine on scent posts at corridor junctures, protruding stones in trails, on old stumps, or under trees. Urine of females in mating season smells perfumy.

Fisher clues:

Look for fisher tracks in the woods, where they energetically check out all the snags, large conifers, and areas of boulders or ledge. If tail drag shows, it will be brushy. Fisher may also cover uneaten kill or stash kill in trees. Dens in hollow trees, downed logs, or under larger boulders. Will scent mark, roll on, bite and scratch small hemlock saplings.

Fisher scat composed mostly of hair:

Fisher scat composed of fruit, with some hair:

Breeding: As with most mustelids, the fisher breeds shortly after giving birth, as it has a delayed implantation that can last 10–11 months. Breeding occurs in March and April.

Gaits: See marten.

front rear

RIVER OTTER, *Lutra canadensis*

Overall Track

- Otter feet are webbed, but the webbing is usually more apparent in the hind tracks.
- Toes are teardrop shaped due to the closeness of the nails.
- Sometimes there is tail drag in the track trail.
- Like other mustelids:
  - Placement of toes is asymmetrical, with the slope going toward the inside of the track. The plantar pad also slopes toward the inside.
  - There is a small heel pad on the front foot only.

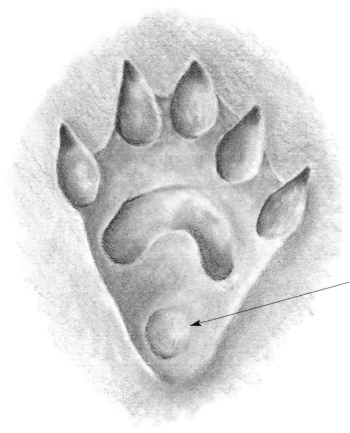

Front Track

Look for heel pad on the front track.

Size: 2 ⅞ to 3 ¼ in. (7.3 to 8.3 cm) long; 1 ⅞ to 3 in. (4.8 to 7.6 cm) wide

Comparisons: Similar to fisher (page 123) and domestic dog (page 117).

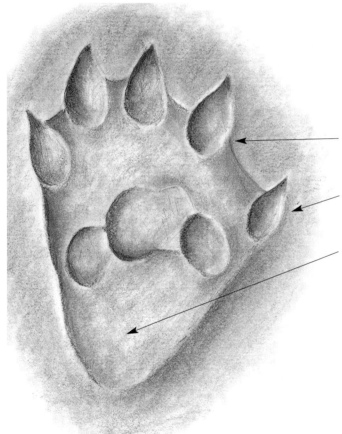

Rear Track

Webbing is more obvious on the hind tracks.

The inner toe often splays way out from the others.

No heel pad shows on the rear track.

Size: 3 to 4 in. (7.6 to 10.2 cm) long; 2 ¼ to 3 ¼ in. (5.7 to 8.3 cm) wide. When toes splay the track can be up to 4 in. (10.2 cm) wide.

front rear

River otter clues:

If tail drag shows, it will be a thick line, not brushy. Look for slides on slopes near bodies of water. Slides are made when the otter sleds on its belly, creating a trough, sometimes pushing with its feet. The otter will slide nearly anywhere it can, including down slopes of snow, down mud into water, and across ice and snow. Otters rub and roll on grasses and in sand as a part of grooming, play, and for scent marking. Look for grass twists (sometimes with scat left nearby), rolled-on vegetation, and depressions with scat deposited on the edge. Otters are very playful, intelligent, and curious animals and leave a very interesting trail to follow.

Trail width: 4 to 8 in. (10.2 to 20.3 cm)

Habitat: In and near lakes, rivers, and ponds, though the otter travels overland from one body of water to another.

Food: Fish are the main food; otters will also eat crustaceans, shellfish, frogs and toads, small mammals, birds, insects, and small amounts of plant material.

Scat: Often a scattered pile of fish scales and bones, or crustacean parts. Smells of fish. Can also be a blob of dark, mucousy material. Also deposits a white, mucouslike material.

Breeding: December to May, usually peaking in the north in March or April. As with most mustelids, otters have a delayed implantation. This delay can be for 8–9 ½ months.

Gaits: See marten. Most common gaits are the loping patterns.

Otter grass twist with scat deposit

Otter slide in snow

STRIPED SKUNK, *Mephitis mephitis*

Overall Track

• Skunk tracks are very delicate in appearance.

Front Track

Nails are well ahead of the toes.

Size:1 ⅞ to 2 ³⁄₁₆ in. (4.8 to 5.6 cm) long; 1 to 1 ⅛ in. (2.5 to 2.9 cm) wide

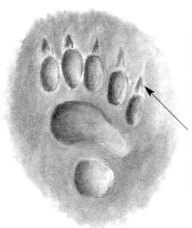

Rear Track

Looks like a tiny human print with nails. The track is reversed from a human print, however, so that the small toe is on the inside.

Nails on the rear track will be much closer to the toes than on the front foot.

Size: 1 ¾ to 2 in. (4.4 to 5.1 cm) long; 1 to 1 ⅛ in (2.5 to 2.9 cm) wide

Trail width: 2 ¾ to 4 ¼ in. (7 to 10.8 cm)

Habitat: Agricultural areas, grassy fields, brush, ravines and ditches, hedgerows, developed areas near agricultural or mixed-use lands.

Food: During spring and summer skunks eat primarily insects (beetles and grubs, especially) and small mammals. In fall and winter fruit becomes important to their diet.

Scat: Scat is often black and composed of indigestible insect parts.

Striped skunk clues:

Striped skunks are often found around buildings. They will use the ground dens of other animals for shelter in winter and when raising young but will use above ground shelter otherwise. In winter they may share a communal den. Gait patterns are often erratic.

Breeding: Mid-February to mid-April

Walk:

Lope:

When faced with a threat a skunk will do a handstand and throw its tail forward. It will also stomp and pound the ground with its front feet, and as a last resort it will turn around and spray.

front rear

HOUSECAT, *Felis catus*

Overall Track

- Housecats are the smallest of the cats, and their tracks are smaller than a bobcat. A young bobcat may have tracks similar in size to a housecat.
- Like other cats:
  - The track is a round compression shape.
  - The front track is more asymmetrical than the rear.
  - Often the nails do not show in the tracks.
  - The plantar pad is blunted or rounded on the leading edge, with two lobes, and cants to the outside.

Front Track

The second toe from the inside usually leads the track.

Toes are somewhat more rounded than on the rear track.

Size: 1 to 1 ⅝ in. (2.5 to 4.1 cm) long; 1 to 1 ¾ in (2.5 to 4.4 cm) wide

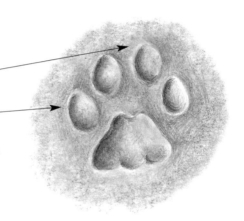

Rear Track

Toes are elongated more on rear.

Plantar pad is often concave on the sides and is taller and narrower than the front track planter pad.

Size: 1 to 1 ⅝ in. (2.5 to 4.1 cm) long; 1 to 1 ¾ in. (2.5 to 4.4 cm) wide

Trail Width: 2 ⅜ to 4 ⅞. (6 to 12.4 cm)

Comparisons: Similar to bobcat (page 124); gray fox (page 119).

Housecat, Bobcat, Lynx, and Mountain Lion Track Patterns

Felids will direct-register walk or trot and can also walk with rears falling behind or ahead of fronts. Housecats can pace, but it is not a common gait.

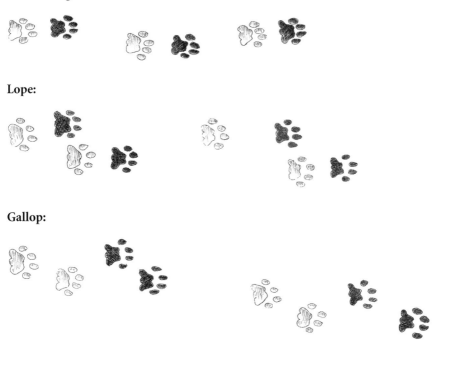

Direct-register walk or trot:

Indirect-register walk:

Each of these is two tracks:
a front track with a rear superimposed on top of it.

Indirect-register trot:

Lope:

Gallop:

BOBCAT, *Lynx rufus*

Overall Track

- Like other cats:
  - The track is a round compression shape.
  - The front track is more asymmetrical than the rear.
  - Often the nails do not show in the tracks.
  - The plantar pad is blunted or rounded on the leading edge, with two lobes, and cants to the outside.

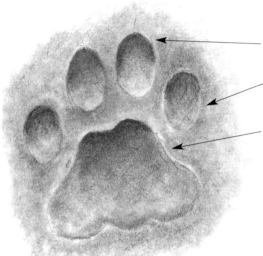

Front Track

The second toe from the inside usually lead the track.

Toes are somewhat more rounded than on the rear track.

The plantar pad on the front is steeper than on the rear, and the toes are closer to the plantar pad.

Size: 1 ⅝ to 2 ½ in. (4.1 to 6.4 cm) long; 1 ½ to 2 ⅝ in. (3.8 to 6.7 cm) wide

Rear Track

Toes are elongated more on the rear.

There is more negative space between toes and plantar pad on the rear track than on the front.

Size: 1 ⅝ to 2 ½ in. (4.1 cm to 6.4 cm) long; 1 ½ to 2 ⅝ in. (3.8 cm to 6.7 cm) wide

Comparisons: Similar to housecat (page 124); fisher (page 125); mountain lion and lynx (page 126).

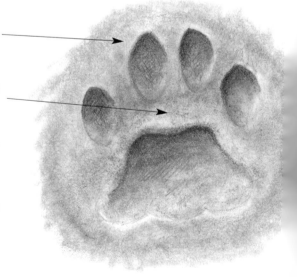

Trail width: 3 to 5 ⅜ in. (7.6 to 13.7 cm)

Habitat: Uses a wide variety of habitats, including wetlands, mixed habitats, and mountainous areas. Rests and dens around rocky ledges and conifer swamps. Uses roads and trails frequently.

Food: Snowshoe hare, cottontail rabbit, squirrels, mice, voles, and other small and medium-sized mammals, as well as birds, reptiles, and insects.

> **Bobcat clues:**
>
> Look for south-facing, ledgy areas in winter where bobcats like to lie in the sun.

Scat and urine: Scat is segmented, most often blunt on the ends, and full of hair. It is often deposited in a scrape but only sometimes covered. Will scent mark by spraying urine on objects.

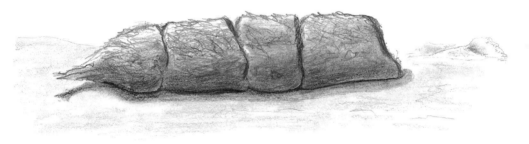

Breeding: February and March.

Track patterns: See housecat.

front rear

LYNX, *Lynx canadensis*

Overall Track

- Lynx tracks are distinctive in that they have very small toe and plantar pads in relation to the overall print.
- Lynx have very furry feet and will show a lot of hair; the compression will often extend outward much further than the toes and plantar pad.
- Like other cats:
  - The track is a round compression shape.
  - The front track is more asymmetrical than the rear.
  - Often the nails do not show in the tracks.
  - The plantar pad is blunted or rounded on the leading edge, with two lobes, and cants to the outside.

Size: 3 ¼ to 3 ¾ in. (8.3 to 9.5 cm) long; 3 to 3 ⅜ in. (7.6 to 8.6 cm) wide

Front Track

Toes spread more on the front track, and there is a leading toe.

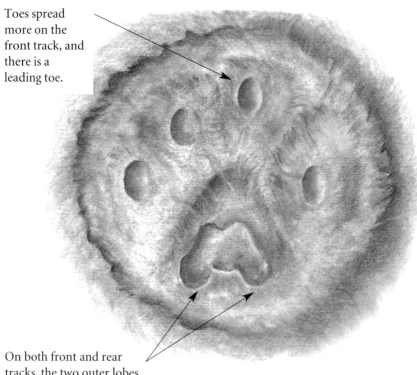

On both front and rear tracks, the two outer lobes on the plantar pad extend below the middle lobe.

Rear Track

Size: The rear track is slightly larger than the front track when toes are spread.

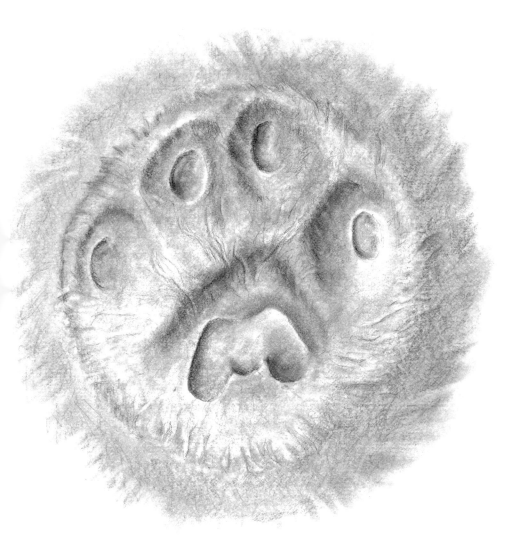

Comparisons: Similar to mountain lion and bobcat (page 126).

Trail width: 6 ¼ to 9 in. (15.9 to 22.9 cm)

Habitat: The lynx dwells in boreal forests, inhabiting areas with deep snow. Prefers dense conifer forests interspersed with patches of early successional hardwood, wetlands, and thickets.

Food: Mainly snowshoe hare, but occasionally other small mammals and birds.

Scat and urine: Scat is often full of hare fur. Lynx will use urine to scent mark.

> **Lynx clues:**
>
> Lynx tracks in mud or moist snow will show the toes and hair, with lots of negative space between the toes and heel pad. Lynx tracks in snow will show a large compression shape with toes and plantar pads obscured.

Breeding: February and March.

*Note: Information regarding lynx and lynx tracks provided by Susan C. Morse.[3]

Track Patterns

See housecat for basic track patterns. In addition, Sue Morse, professional tracker and wildlife habitat specialist, has researched a unique lynx gait that separates it from other felids. Morse has found that lynx often move just like their primary prey, the snowshoe hare, in the typical rabbit jump.

front rear

MOUNTAIN LION, *Felis concolor*

Overall Track

- Look for the large toes in comparison to the plantar pad. In certain rare situations the dewclaw may show.
- Toes are teardrop shaped, and the outer toe is smaller than the others.
- Like other cats:
  - The track is a round compression shape.
  - The front track is more asymmetrical than the rear.
  - Often the nails do not show in the tracks.
  - The plantar pad is blunted or rounded on the leading edge, with two lobes, and cants to the outside.

Front Track

The second toe from the inside usually lead the track, making the front track more asymmetrical than the rear track.

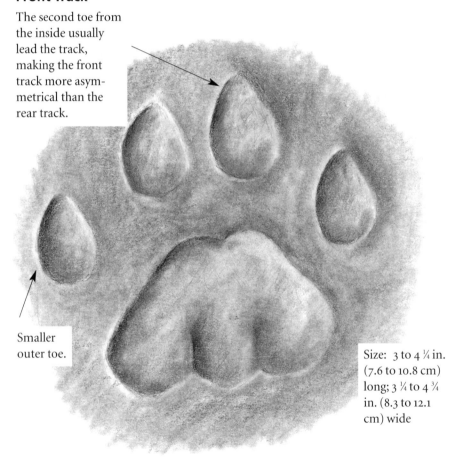

Smaller outer toe.

Size: 3 to 4 ¼ in. (7.6 to 10.8 cm) long; 3 ¼ to 4 ¾ in. (8.3 to 12.1 cm) wide

Comparisons: Similar to lynx and bobcat (page 126); dog and wolf (page 115).

Rear Track

The rear track is slightly smaller and less asymmetrical than the front track.

Smaller outer toe.

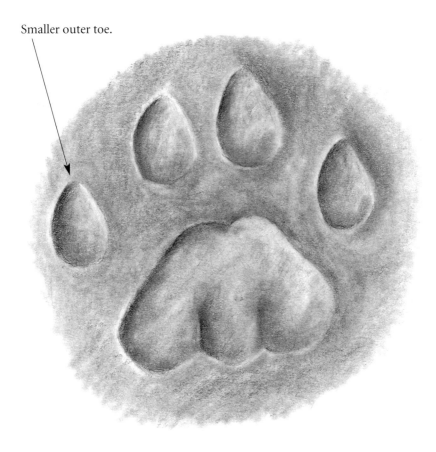

Trail width: 8 to 11 in. (20.3 to 28 cm)

Habitat: The native habitat of the Eastern mountain lion, or cougar, was a mosaic forest of woods and open areas, with wetlands nearby. Now an endangered species in the eastern United States. Occasional sightings of mountain lion in the Northeast justify its inclusion in this field guide.

Mountain lion clues:

Many tracks believed to be mountain lion are domestic dog tracks.

Food: Principle prey is deer.

Scat and urine: Scat resembles wolf in size but will segment like bobcat scat. Mountain lion will sometimes use scat to scent mark and will scrape up small dirt piles of forest debris and urinate on them as scent posts.

Breeding: Mountain lions breed any time of the year.

Gaits: See housecat.

Mountain lion covering kill

front rear

WHITE-TAILED DEER, *Odocoileus virginianus*

Overall Track

- The white-tail's track can be heart-shaped, or the toes can spread out. The front track illustration shows the heart shape, while the rear track illustration shows the toes spread out, but either foot can have the toes together or spread.
- Dewclaws may or may not show.

The front and rear tracks will be about the same size.

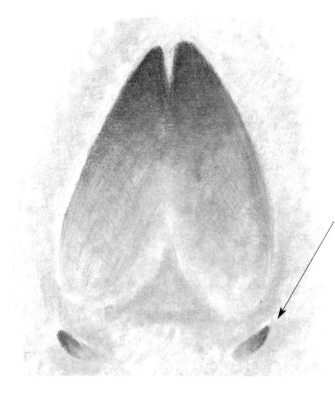

Front Track

The front and rear tracks are similar. If dewclaws show, the ones on the front will point outwards and be closer in to the toes than on the rear.

Size: 1 ¼ to 3 ½ in. (3.2 to 8.9 cm) long; 1 ⅜ to 2 ⅞ in. (3.5 to 7.3 cm) wide

Comparisons: Similar to elk (page 127).

Rear Track

If dewclaws show on the rear, they will point straight and be farther away from the toes than the dewclaws on the front.

Size: 1 ¼ to 3 ½ in. (3.2 to 8.9 cm) long; 1 ⅜ to 2 ⅞ in. (3.5 to 7.3 cm) wide

Browse is torn rather than cut

Antler rubs from deer are usually low on a sapling

"Barking" on tree. If higher than shoulder height then the barking is from moose.

front rear

Trail width: 5 to 11 ½ in. (12.7 to 29.2 cm)

Habitat: Occurs in a variety of habitats but thrives in early mixed successional stages, including suburban and agricultural areas.

Food: Deer graze on grasses, forbs, and the new leaves of woody plants when available. They feed heavily on acorns, beechnuts, and other mast. They also browse on buds and twigs throughout winter.

> **Deer clues:**
>
> Look for deer beds, runs and conifer deer yards where they gather in herds for winter. Deer browse is torn, due to deer having only bottom incisors on their front lower jaw and a hard pad on top. Deer will "bark" trees (scrape them with bottom incisors), and bucks will rub small trees with antlers and forehead. Bucks also make scrapes with their front feet along runs, and all deer dig through the snow and forest litter to access acorns and green grasses. Antlers may be found when they are dropped after breeding season.

Scat and urine: Scat are oblong pellets with points on one end and often a dimple at the other. They are deposited in groups. Individual pellets are usually no more than one half inch (1.3 cm) in diameter; moose scat is much larger. When feeding on green vegetation, deer pellets can be in a loose patty. Deer urine in winter smells very piney. Deer feeding on acorns will have dark red-brown urine.

Breeding: Late fall.

Deer, Moose, and Elk Track Patterns

Ungulates can do a direct- or indirect-register trot and walk.

Walks and trots:

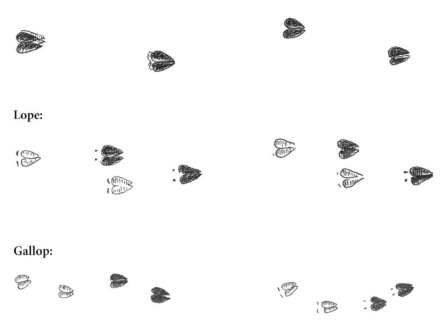

Lope:

Gallop:

Pronk or stot: In addition to the gaits shown above, white-tailed deer will also do a gait known as a pronk or stot, a kind of jump in which the front feet land ahead of and at the same time as the rear feet.

front rear

ELK OR WAPITI, *Cervus elaphus*

Front and Rear Track

- Two-toed compression, with each toe being somewhat bean-shaped. Overall track is less heart-shaped than deer or moose. Dewclaws may or may not show.

Size: 3 ⅛ to 4 ⅞ in. (7.9 to 12.4 cm) long; 3 ⅛ to 4 ⅝ in. (7.9 to 11.7 cm) wide

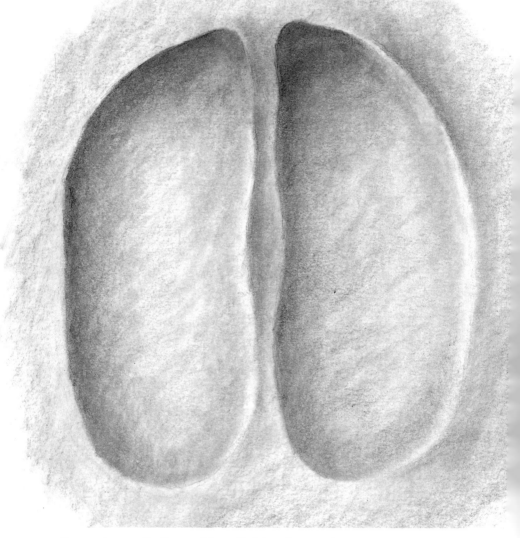

Comparisons: Similar to white-tailed deer (page 127).

Trail width: 7 to 11 in. (17.8 to 27.9 cm)

Habitat: Originally the elk or wapiti were distributed throughout west-central New England, New York, and the south, as well as across other parts of the United States. They were extirpated in the East but reintroduced in Pennsylvania in the early 1900s. A small herd exists there still. In summer they occupy areas of aspen/hardwood forests with openings, and in winter they move to wetlands with forest and openings nearby.

Elk clues:

Look for rut pits or wallows and antler rubs, and antlers that have fallen off after breeding season.

Food: Woody and herbaceous plants.

Scat and urine: Scat resembles that of moose but are smaller. During the rut urine is deposited in wallow pits, and the males roll in it as an attractant to female elk.

Breeding: Mid-September through mid-October.

Track patterns: See white-tailed deer.

front rear

MOOSE, *Alces alces*

Overall Track

- Adult moose tracks are larger than white-tail deer, which they resemble in appearance.
- Moose tracks may appear heart-shaped, or the two toes may be separated, or splayed out.
- Moose calves and yearlings can have a track that resembles the deer in size as well as shape.
- Assume any track over 4 in. long (10.2 cm.) is a moose track, if it is within the geographic distribution of moose in the Northeast.

Front and Rear Track

Both front and rear tracks have two toes, and dewclaws may or may not show.

Size: 4 to 6 ⅞ in. (10.2 to 17.5 cm) long; 3 ½ to 5 ¾ in. (8.9 to 14.6 cm) wide

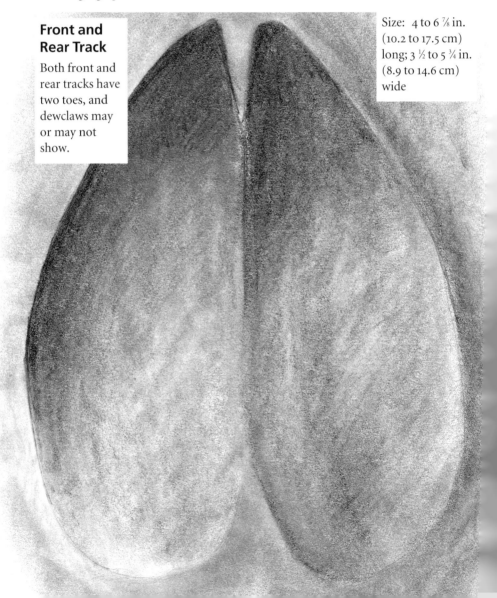

Trail width: 8 ½ to 16 in. (21.6 to 40.6 cm)

Habitat: Boreal (northern) forests. Prefers coniferous forest, swamps and other wetlands, aspen thickets, and willow/aspen areas.

Food: Browse in winter (favored species are balsam fir, willow, aspen, and birch, but they will eat many species); aquatic plants in summer.

Scat and urine: Scat are blockier than deer scat, and larger. In winter, when moose are eating browse, the scat are usually in separate pellets. When they eat succulent vegetation, the scat is more of a large patty. Bulls in rut will urinate in rut pits and roll in them.

Moose clues:

Look for moose tracks in late spring, summer, and early fall near wetlands, rivers, and ponds. In winter they move upland. Also look for wallows or pits made by the bulls in mating season (rut); barking scrapes on trees (shoulder height and above), particularly red maples; antler rubs and damaged trees in fall with antler marks on them; and antlers that have fallen off after breeding season. Also look for browse on balsam fir and other plant species.

Breeding: Mid-September through October with a peak in the last week of September and first week of October.

Track patterns: See white-tailed deer. Moose have much longer strides than deer.

Comparison Pages

Shrew	Vole	Mouse (Peromyscus spp.)

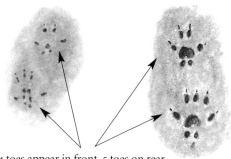

5 toes, front and rear.

4 toes appear in front, 5 toes on rear in voles and mice

Other things to look for:

- Will usually walk or shuffle.

- Narrow trail width compared to voles or mice—one inch (2.5 cm) or less.

- In winter shrews make tunnels under the surface of the snow to travel.

- Carnivorous.

Other things to look for:

- Can jump but usually walks or shuffles.

- Most species of voles have a trail width larger than shrews—1 to 1 ⅝ in. (2.5 to 4.1 cm).

- In winter voles make tunnels under the surface of the snow to travel in. In summer they make their runways in tall grasses.

- Omnivorous.

Other things to look for:

- Can walk but most often jumps.

- Tail drag sometimes seen in trail.

- Travels above the surface of the snow more often than shrews or voles.

- Omnivorous and makes middens of nut and seed shells.

Snowshoe Hare   ## Cottontail Rabbit

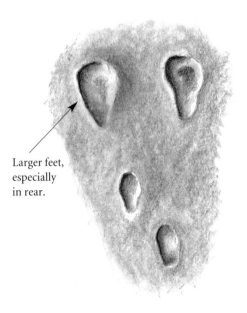

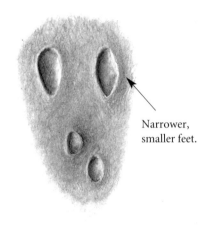

Larger feet, especially in rear.

Narrower, smaller feet.

Other things to look for:

- Snowshoe hare habitat is forested and brushy areas, where there is access to conifers; also wetland areas.

Other things to look for:

- Eastern cottontail habitat is open farmland, residential areas, thickets, and swampy woods. They are rarely found in heavy forest. However, New England cottontails will be found in dense forests where there is shrub cover.

Gray Squirrel

Look for:

- Trail width is 3 ½–5 ½ inches (8.9–14 cm). Any group of tracks over 4 ¼ inches (10.8 cm) wide can be considered gray squirrel.

- In a very clear track you can see the more bulbous toes of the gray squirrel.

- Gray squirrels prefer deciduous forests, parks, and suburbs.

Red Squirrel

Look for:

- Trail width is 3–4 ¼ inches (7.6–10.8 cm). Any group of winter tracks with trail width less than 3 ½ inches (8.9 cm) can be considered red or flying squirrel (summer tracks of that size could be chipmunk).

- In a very clear track you can see the longer and less bulbous toes of the red squirrel.

- Red squirrels prefer coniferous or mixed coniferous and deciduous forests.

Note: Flying squirrel tracks and trail width can overlap gray squirrel, red squirrel, and chipmunks. The only way to distinguish flying squirrels from other squirrels and the chipmunk is a clear trail where front and rear tracks can be distinguished from one another. If the fronts fall ahead of the rears fairly often as it jumps, it is likely to be a flying squirrel. Also, if you are sure a track was made during the daytime, you can rule out a southern flying squirrel, as they are nocturnal. Northern flying squirrels are primarily nocturnal but occasionally emerge during daylight.

Eastern Chipmunk

Look for:

- Trail width is 2 ⅛–3 ⅛ inches (5.4–7.9 cm). This is usually smaller than most red squirrels and larger than voles and mice.

- Chipmunks go into torpor for winter, and their tracks are rarely seen then.

Deer Mouse, White-footed Mouse, Jumping Mouse, Vole spp.

Look for:

- Trail widths of mice and voles are 1–1 ¾ inches (2.5–4.4 cm). These are smaller than the Eastern chipmunk.

Squirrel

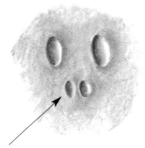

Squirrels will have their front tracks side by side or at a slight angle more often than rabbits or hares.

Rabbit and Hare

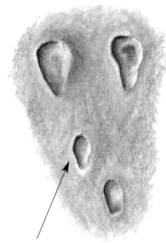

Rabbits and hares will have a far leading front track or one front track behind the other more often than squirrels.

Other things to look for:

- Squirrel tracks most often end at trees or go back and forth between trees.

- Squirrels leave debris and middens of broken nut shells, conifer cones, and hemlock nip twigs.

- Squirrels leave very small cylindrical pellets as scat.

Other things to look for:

- Rabbits and hares don't form runs between trees.

- Often rabbit and hare tracks are found in brushy areas where squirrels are not found (unless there are trees nearby).

- Rabbits and hares make 45-degree cuts on low twigs and vegetation.

- Rabbits and hares leave very round pellets as scat.

Deer Mouse, White-footed Mouse

All four tracks are about the same size.

Deer mice and white-footed mice place their front feet behind their rears when jumping.

Other things to look for:

- Deer mouse and white-footed mouse tracks can be found in winter, as they are active year-round.

Woodland Mouse, Meadow Jumping Mouse

Rear tracks are longer than front tracks.

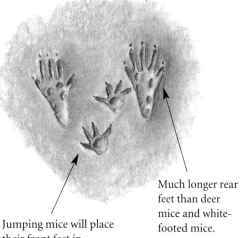

Much longer rear feet than deer mice and white-footed mice.

Jumping mice will place their front feet in between or in front of their rear feet more often than deer mice and white-footed mice when jumping.

Other things to look for:

- Jumping mouse tracks will not be found in winter, as they hibernate.

Gray Wolf	**Domestic Dog**	**Coyote**
Larger than most dog tracks; larger than coyote.	Dog toes often splay out more than coyote.	Coyotes hold their toes tight together, and often the nails on the outside toes do not show.

Note: Dog, wolf, and coyote tracks can appear very similar and are very difficult to tell apart. The most distinguishing characteristic of the dog and the coyote is the trail each animal leaves behind.

Other things to look for:

- Gray wolf tracks average 4 inches (10.2 cm) long.

- Wolves often kill large animals such as moose, whereas coyotes kill smaller animals such as rabbits and occasionally deer. Coyotes will scavenge wolf kills, however, so their tracks may be found near kill sites.

Other things to look for:

- In a study done by James Halfpenny, Darren Ireland, Lara Bonn, and Kiann Thompson, medium- to large-sized dog front tracks averaged 3.4 inches (8.6 cm) in length.[4]

- Domestic dogs often make very erratic trails as they run around in the woods and fields. However, feral dogs may have tracks and trails indistinguishable from coyotes.

- Scat of domestic dogs are usually very grainy and have few hairs or bone fragments in them. Feral dogs will have scat indis-tinguishable from coyotes. Dogs deposit scat randomly.

Other things to look for:

- Eastern coyote tracks are 2 ⅞–3 ½ inches (7.3 to 8.9 cm) long.

- Coyotes make very straight, businesslike trails, unless they are engaged in play or courtship.

- Scat of coyotes are usually filled with hair and bits of bone or fruit, or are dark masses from eating organ meat. Coyotes leave their scat in the middle of trails and prefer to leave them on high points of trails or on stones in the trail.

Domestic Dog (or Wolf) Mountain Lion

In the east, many reports of mountain lion tracks are actually domestic dog tracks. Dog tracks are highly variable. If a dog twists its foot at all when placing it, it can make an asymmetrical track like a felid. Below is an illustration of a dog track that might be mistaken for a lion, with a blurred leading edge of plantar pad. However, if the leading edge is clear, it will be much more pointed.

Usually some impressions of nails will show and they will be blunt and thick.

Will rarely show a leading toe.

Will regularly show a leading toe on the front track.

Most often nails will not show. If they do show, the nails will be narrow and sharply pointed.

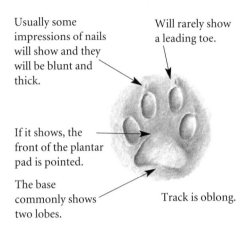

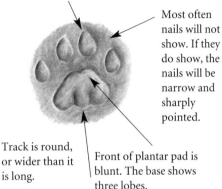

If it shows, the front of the plantar pad is pointed.

The base commonly shows two lobes.

Track is oblong.

Track is round, or wider than it is long.

Front of plantar pad is blunt. The base shows three lobes.

Other things to look for:

- Dogs will do an oblique trot.

- Dogs often leave a wandering trail. Wolves make straighter trails, like mountain lions.

- Dog scat will be grainy if the dog is not feral or feeding on wild game. Wolf scat may be very similar to mountain lion.

Other things to look for:

- Mountain lions do not do an oblique trot.

- Mountain lions leave a straight trail.

- Will cover a kill.

- Scat will often be more segmented than that of a dog and will contain hair and bone fragments or will be very dark and smooth from feeding on organ meat.

- May make a urine-soaked scrape or leave scat in a scrape.

> **Note:** In 1988, researchers K. Shawn Smallwood and E. Lee Fitzhugh published the findings of a study in which they examined the commonly used criteria for discriminating between lion and dog tracks and then measured all of the variables with the tracks of the two different species. (Their research was done in mud or dust but not snow.) What they found was that the most accurate discriminator was the angle of the long axis of the outer toes with respect to each other. The criteria about the tracks themselves noted above were other accurate traits.[5]

Coyote

Doglike appearance.

Red Fox

Often has an arrowhead appearance.

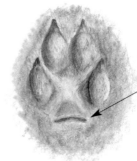

A bar or chevron can be found in the front track plantar pad of the red fox.

Other things to look for:

- Track is 2 ½–3 inches (6.4 to 7.6 cm) long. Larger track than red fox.

- Strides on paired gaits that are over 19 inches (48.3 cm) are more likely to be coyote than red fox. Coyotes can do shorter strides, but red fox generally don't go over 19 inches.[6]

- Urine markings do not smell skunky.

Other things to look for:

- Track is 1 ¾ –2 ½ inches (4.4 to 6.6 cm) long. Smaller track than coyote.

- Urine markings will smell strongly like skunk.

Domestic Dog   River Otter

Domestic dog and otter tracks can look similar, especially if the inner toe and webbing of the otter doesn't show.

Usually a symmetrical track.

Asymmetrical, even if the fifth toe doesn't show.

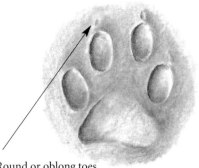

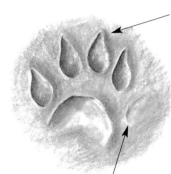

Toes and nails are often joined in the track and make the toes look teardrop-shaped.

Round or oblong toes with very chunky nails that often show as separated from toe compressions.

If inner toe appears, it will be smaller than the other toes.

Other things to look for:

- If an animal consistently does a coupled track pattern such as that of a walk or trot, it will be a canid. If the print is otter sized, it will be a dog or a coyote.

- Will roll in the snow but will not make slides like otters.

- Some dogs may show webbing in their tracks between the toes, but it will be lower down on the toes.

Other things to look for:

- If an animal very rarely does a coupled track pattern, instead doing a more consistent lope or bound, it will be an otter or fisher.

- If the animal makes slides in its trail, or into water, it is likely to be an otter.

- Otters have webbing between all toes, though sometimes it will not show clearly.

Red Fox

Gray Fox

Arrowhead-shaped track.

Rounder track, close to that of a cat.

Nails will show.

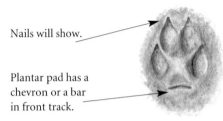

Nails may or may not show.

Plantar pad has a chevron or a bar in front track.

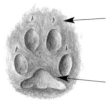

Plantar pad is shallow with a rounded lobe.

Fur on the feet register in the track.

Feet are not as furry as red fox, so a clearer print often appears.

Other things to look for:

- Urine smells strong, skunky.

- Found in all parts of the Northeast.

Other things to look for:

- Urine has only faint smell of skunk.

- Can climb trees.

- Not found in northern Maine (see range map for gray fox).

Gray Fox

Housecat

Symmetrical track.

Asymmetrical track with leading toe, especially in front track.

Nails will show more often than on a cat.

Plantar pad shape is flat and shallow, and the top is rounded with no lobes.

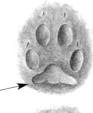

Nails often don't show.

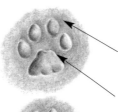

Second toe leads the track.

Plantar pad is steep, with two lobes at the top.

Rear track may show very little of the plantar pad.

Rear plantar pad will usually show fully in the track.

Rear track is smaller than the front track.

Rear track is close to the same size as the front track.

Other things to look for:

- An X can be drawn through the gray fox's tracks, owing to the symmetry and placement of the outer toes in relation to the inner toes.

- A line drawn across the tops of the outer toes will not usually bisect either of the inner toes.

Other things to look for:

- The negative space between the toes and plantar pad on cats is more of a C shape.

- A line drawn across the tops of the outer toes will usually bisect or cut through at least one of the inner toes.

Mink   Long-tailed Weasel

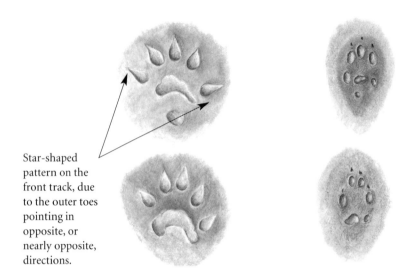

Star-shaped pattern on the front track, due to the outer toes pointing in opposite, or nearly opposite, directions.

A female mink and a male long-tailed weasel may have tracks of similar size, and both species use similar gaits. However, the weasel will most often use a bound in snow, and the mink will vary its gait to include the bound and the three- and four-track loping patterns.

Mink   Marten

Mink may be found inhabiting areas where there are marten, but marten have a limited range, mostly in the farthest northern parts of the Northeast in unbroken coniferous forests. Mink, however, are found in many areas of the Northeast and live primarily in areas where there are wetlands or other bodies of water.

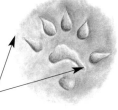

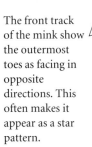

The front track of the mink show the outermost toes as facing in opposite directions. This often makes it appear as a star pattern.

Marten feet are generally furrier than mink feet, but in summer they lose some of the fur, making it more difficult to distinguish the species.

Other things to look for:

- Mink primarily hunt around bodies of water.

- Mink are not arboreal animals.

Other things to look for:

- Marten hunt primarily in the forest.

- Marten are very much arboreal animals and tracks will often lead to trees.

Fisher

Marten

The fisher's feet are not as heavily furred as its cousin the marten, and in winter clear prints may be found.

Below is the summer print of the marten. In winter, the print is much less sharp due to more fur on the bottom of the foot.

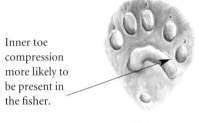

Inner toe compression more likely to be present in the fisher.

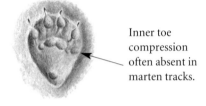

Inner toe compression often absent in marten tracks.

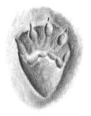

Other things to look for:

- Fisher can be found where marten live but also live where marten are absent, namely in second-growth forests and farther south. Check range maps.

Other things to look for:

- Marten are found in a more specific habitat than fisher; they live in mature or old-growth northern spruce and balsam fir mixed forests of the far north.

Otter   Fisher

Otter and fisher can be very hard to distinguish from one another. Often behavior is the best indicator of species.

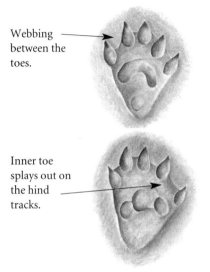

Webbing between the toes.

Inner toe splays out on the hind tracks.

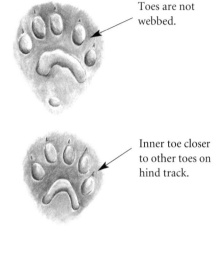

Toes are not webbed.

Inner toe closer to other toes on hind track.

Other things to look for:

- Otters tend to make slides in the snow more frequently than fishers do. Otters also make grass twists.

- Otters are semi-aquatic mammals, and their tracks are most often found near water, though they frequently travel overland. Tracks going into the water are more likely to be otter than fisher.

- Otter tails are smooth rather than fluffy and don't show a brushlike stroke when they appear in a track.

- Scat will most often have fish scales and crayfish remains and will be in a loose pile.

Other things to look for:

- Fishers often move erratically through the forest, hopping up on stumps and checking out lots of trees and rock crevices.

- Fishers will mark and roll on small hemlock saplings.

- Fishers will mark territory with urine scent posts. Female urine can smell like perfume.

- If tail drag shows, it will be a brushlike stroke.

- Scat will be a long cylindrical tube, or narrow, twisted, and tightly packed with fur. Often folds back on itself.

Housecat   # Bobcat

Smaller size than bobcat— 1 to 1 ⅝ inches (2.5 to 4.1 cm) long.

Larger size than housecat— 1 ⅝ to 2 ½ inches (4.1 to 6.4 cm) long.

Other things to look for:

- A delicate print.

- Most domestic (non-feral) housecats will not direct-register walk or trot consistently except in deep snow.

Other things to look for:

- Generally more robust than housecats.

- Will consistently direct-register walk and trot.

Bobcat   Fisher

In certain conditions, fisher and bobcat tracks can resemble one another. This is especially true when the fisher's inner or outer toe is unclear, and/or when the plantar pad is unclear.

Unusual for claw marks to show.

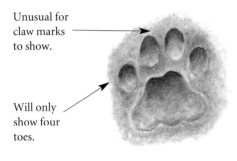

Nails will show.

Will only show four toes.

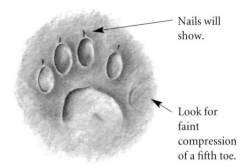

Look for faint compression of a fifth toe.

Other things to look for:

- Bobcats will usually walk or trot.

- Scat are segmented and often blunt on at least one end; composed of hair or fur, bones, or dark mash from organ meat. Bobcats rarely eat anything other than meat.

Other things to look for:

- Fishers will usually lope or bound when moving directly through an area.

- Fishers leave an erratic trail when checking out snags, trees, boulders, and ledges.

- Scat is long and narrow; twisted and tight if it is composed of hair or fur, or tubular if it is composed of fruit, nuts, berries, or dark mash from organ meat. Fishers are primarily carnivores, but will also eat fruit, nuts, or berries.

Mountain Lion   # Lynx

Larger toes and plantar pad in relation to the overall track.

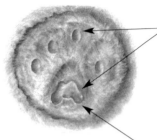

Tiny toes and plantar pad in relation to overall track.

On both front and rear tracks, the two outer lobes at the base of the plantar pad are even with the middle lobe.

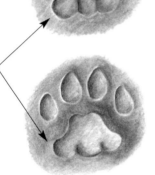

On both front and rear tracks, the two outer lobes at the base of the plantar pad extend below the middle lobe.

Rear foot just slightly smaller than front foot.

Not very heavily furred feet.

Very furry feet.

Rear foot is slightly larger than front foot.

Other things to look for:

- Scat will contain mostly deer hair and bones.

- There is no known breeding population of mountain lions in the northeastern United States but random sightings do occur.

Other things to look for:

- Scat will contain mostly hare fur and bones.

- The only documented lynx population in the northeastern United States is in Maine.

Note: Bobcat tracks are smaller than either of these felids, though they can look very similar.

White-tailed Deer   ## Elk

Toes form a heart-shaped track.   Toes are bean shaped.

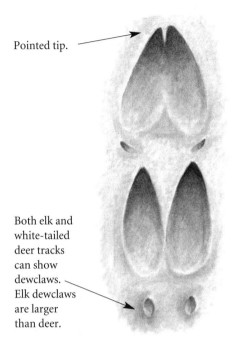
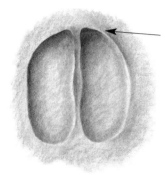
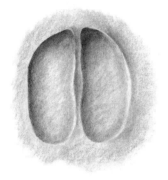

Pointed tip.

Blunt tip.

Both elk and white-tailed deer tracks can show dewclaws. Elk dewclaws are larger than deer.

Other things to look for:

- Smaller than elk tracks.
- Scat is smaller than elk, and when pelletized each pellet is about the size of a large raisin.
- Found throughout the northeastern United States.

Other things to look for:

- Larger than deer tracks.
- Scat is larger than deer, and when pelletized each pellet is about the size of a large olive.
- Only found in a small area of Pennsylvania.

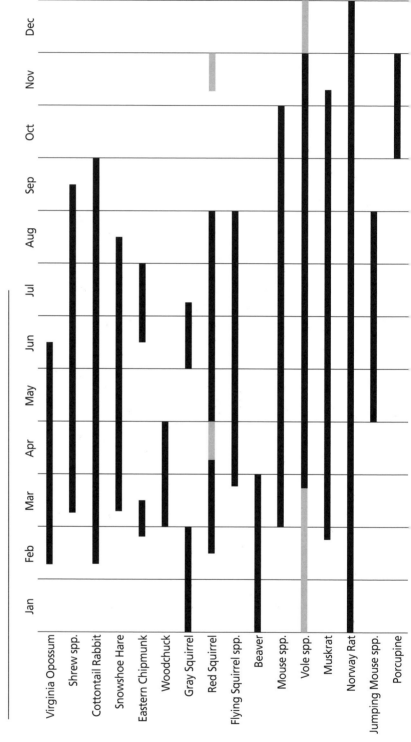

Breeding Seasons in the Northeast

	Jan	Feb	Mar	Apr	May	Jun	Jul	Aug	Sep	Oct	Nov	Dec
Virginia Opossum												
Shrew spp.												
Cottontail Rabbit												
Snowshoe Hare												
Eastern Chipmunk												
Woodchuck												
Gray Squirrel												
Red Squirrel												
Flying Squirrel spp.												
Beaver												
Mouse spp.												
Vole spp.												
Muskrat												
Norway Rat												
Jumping Mouse spp.												
Porcupine												

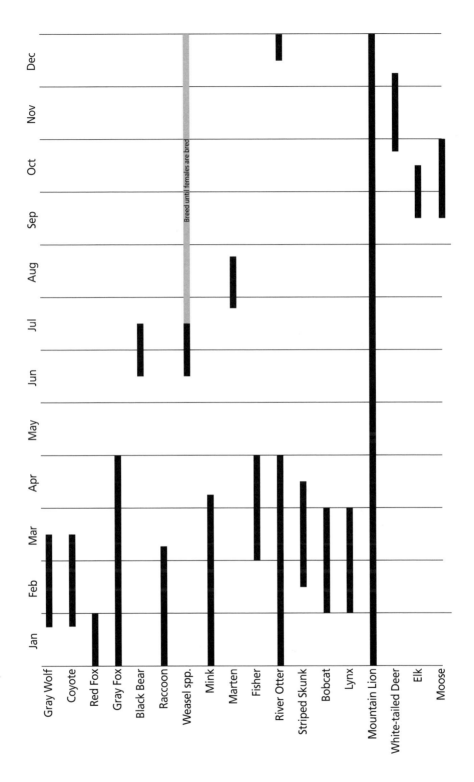

Notes

1. Harrison, D., and T. Chapin, 1998. "Extent and connectivity of habitat for wolves in eastern North America." Wildlife Society Bulletin 26 (4): 767–775.

2. W. Zeilinski and R. Truex, "Distinguishing Tracks of Marten and Fisher at Track-Plate Stations," *Journal of Wildlife Management* 59/3 (1995):571–579

3. S. Morse, personal interview. Also see S. Morse, "An interview with Sue Morse about the Canada Lynx," *The Northern Forest Forum* 8/5 (2000) and "Snow Tracking" by Halfpenny, Thompson, Morse, Holden, and Rezendes, USDA Forest Service General Technical Report PSW-GTR-157, chapter 5 in W. Zeilinski and T. Kucera, eds., *American Marten, Fisher, Lynx, and Wolverine : Survey Methods for Their Detection,* 1995, 12–14.

4. J. Halfpenny, D. Ireland, L. Bonn, and D. Thompson, *Tracking Canids: Track and Trail Synopsis* (Gardiner, Montana: Tracker's Research Association, 1998).

5. K. Smallwood and E. Fitzhugh, "Differentiating Mountain Lion and Dog Tracks," *Proceedings of the Third Mountain Lion Workshop,* Dec. 6–8, 1988 (Prescott, Arizona; Arizona Game and Fish Department, 1989).

6. P. Rezendes, *Tracking & the Art of Seeing: How to Read Animal Tracks and Sign,* 2nd ed. (New York: HarperCollins Publishers, 1999), 201.

Bibliography

General Reference

Bauer, E. *Wild Dogs: The Wolves, Coyotes and Foxes of North America.* San Francisco: Chronicle Books, 1994.

Chapman, J. and G. Feldhamer, eds. *Wild Mammals of North America: Biology, Management, Economics.* Baltimore: Johns Hopkins University Press, 1982.

DeGraaf, R., and M. Yamasaki. *New England Wildlife: Habitat, Natural History and Distribution.* Hanover, New Hampshire: University of New England Press, 2001.

Halfpenny, J. *A Field Guide to Mammal Tracking in North America.* Boulder, Colorado: Johnson Printing Company, 1986.

Henry, J. David. *How to Spot a Fox.* Willowdale, Ontario: Firefly Books Ltd., 1993.

Henry, J. David. *Red Fox: The Catlike Canine.* Washington, D.C.: Smithsonian Institution Press, 1986, 1996.

Merritt, J. *Guide to the Mammals of Pennsylvania.* Pittsburgh: University of Pittsburgh Press, 1987.

Morse, S. "Tracking Tips." *Vermont Woodlands Magazine* (now *Northern Woodlands Magazine*). Corinth, Vt. Summer 1998–spring 2003.

Murie, O. *A Field Guide to Animal Tracks.* Boston: Houghton Mifflin Company, 1954.

Powell, R. *The Fisher: Life History, Ecology and Behavior.* Minneapolis: University of Minnesota Press, 1993.

Rezendes, P. *Tracking & the Art of Seeing: How to Read Animal Tracks and Sign.* 2nd. ed. New York: HarperCollins Publishers, 1999.

Roze, U. *The North American Porcupine.* Washington, D.C.: Smithsonian Institution Press, 1989.

Whitaker, J., and W. Hamilton. *Mammals of the Eastern United States.* Ithaca, New York: Cornell University Press, 1998.

Zielinski, W., and T. Kucera, eds., *American Marten, Fisher, Lynx, and Wolverine: Survey Methods for Their Detection.* USDA Forest Service General Technical Report PSW-GTR-157, 1995.

Gaits

Bang, P., and P. Dahlstrom. *Collins Guide to Animal Tracks and Sign.* London: Wm. Collins Sons and Co. Ltd., 1974.

Halfpenny, J. *A Field Guide to Mammal Tracking in North America.* Boulder, Colorado: Johnson Printing Company, 1986.

Hildebrand, M. *Analysis of Vertebrate Structure.* Boston: John Wiley and Sons, 1974.

Mybridge, E. *Animals in Motion.* Mineola; New York: Dover Publications, 1957.

Rezendes, P. *Tracking & the Art of Seeing: How to Read Animal Tracks and Sign.* 2nd. ed. New York: HarperCollins Publishers, 1999.

Pressure Releases

Brown, *The Science and Art of Tracking: Nature's Path to Spiritual Discovery.* New York: Berkeley Publishing Group, 1999.

Index

Page numbers in *italics* represent comparison pages.

Alces alces, 106–107
Antler rub, 101, 105, 107
Asymmetry, 5

Bank dens or bank burrows, 39, 45, 75
Bar, or chevron, 5, 60
Barking, 101, 102, 107
Bear, Black, 66–69
Beaver, 36–39
Blarina brevicauda, 20–21
Bobcat, 90–91, *124, 125, 126*
       track patterns, 89
Breeding season chart, 128–129

Caching, 31, 41, 62, 73, 75, 81
Canis
       familiaris, 52–53, *114, 115, 117*
       latrans, 58–59, *114, 116*
       lupus, 54–57, *114*
Castor canadensis, 36–39
Castoreum, 39
Cervus elaphus, 104–105, *127*
Chipmunk, Eastern, 26–27, *111*
Clethriomomys gapperi, 42–43
Compressions, 15
Cottontail
       Eastern, 22–23, *110, 112*
       New England, 22–23, *110, 112*
Cougar. *See* Mountain Lion
Coyote, 58–59, *114, 116*
       track patterns, 57

Dams, 38, 39
Didelphis virginiana, 18–19
Deer, White-tailed, 100–102, *127*
       track patterns, 103
Dewclaws, 7, 100, 101, 104, 106
Direct register, 5, 8

Dog, domestic, 52–53, *114, 115, 117*
       track patterns, 57

Elk, 104–105, *127*
       track patterns, 103
Erethizon dorsatum, 50–51

Felis
       catus, 88, *119, 124*
       concolor, 96–99, *115, 126*
Fisher, 80–81, *122, 123, 125*
       track patterns, 79
Forms, 23, 25
Fox
       Gray, 64–65, *118, 119*
              track patterns, 63
       Red, 60–62, *116, 118*
              track patterns, 63

Gaits and track patterns, defined
       bound, 9–10
       gallop, 8–9
       jump, 8–9
       lope, 8–9
       oblique trot, 8
       pace, 7–8
       pronk, 103
       stot, 103
       trot, 7–8
       walk, 7–8
Glaucomys
       sabrinus, 34–35, *111*
       volans, 34–35, *111*
Grass twists, 84

Hare, Snowshoe, 24–25, *110, 112*
Hibernation, 29, 49. *See also* Torpor

Housecat, 88, *119, 124*
    track patterns, 89
Humanlike print, 6

Indirect register, 5, 6

Key, 11–14

Lepus americanus, 24–25, *110, 112*
Lodges, 38, 39, 45, 75
Lutra canadensis, 82–85, *117, 123*
Lynx, 92–95, *126*
    track patterns, 89
Lynx
    canadensis, 92–95, *126*
    rufus, 90–91, 124, 125, *126*

Marmota monax, 28–29
Marten, 76–78 *121, 122*
    track patterns, 79
Martes
    americana, 76–78 *121, 122*
    pennanti, 80–81, *122, 123, 125*
Measuring tracks, 10
Mephitis mephitis, 86–87
Microtus
    chrotorrhinus, 42–43
    pennsylvanicus, 42–43
    pinetorum, 42–43
Middens, 33, 41
Mink, 74–75, *120, 121*
    track patterns, 79
Moose, 106–107
    track patterns, 103
Mountain Lion, 96–99, *115, 126*
    track patterns, 89
Mouse
    Deer, 40–41, *109, 111, 113*
    Meadow Jumping, 48–49, *113*
    White-footed, 40–41, *109, 111, 113*
    Woodland Jumping , 48–49, *113*
Muskrat, 44–45
Mustela
    erminea, 72–73
    frenata, 72–73, *120*
    nivalis, 72–73
    vison, 74–75, *120, 121*

Napaeozapus insignis, 48–49

Negative space, 5
Nip twigs, 31, 33, 51

Odocoileus virginianus, 100–102, *127*
Ondatra zibethicus, 44–45
Opossum, Virginia, 18–19
Otter, River, 82–85, *117, 123*
    track patterns, 79

Pads, 6
Peromyscus
    leucopus, 40–41, *109, 111, 114*
    maniculatus, 40–41, *109, 111, 114*
Porcupine, 50–51
Procyon lotor, 70–71

Raccoon, 70–71
Rat, Norway, 46–47
Rattus norvegicus, 46–47

Scent marking or scat posts, 53, 56, 59, 62, 65,
    75, 78, 81, 84, 91, 94, 98
Scent mounds, 39
Sciurus carolinensis, 30–31, *111, 112*
Shrews
    Masked, 20–21
    N. Short-tailed, 20–21, *109*
    Pygmy, 20–21
    Smoky, 20–21
    Water, 20–21
Skunk, Striped, 86–87
Slides, 75, 84, 85
Snowshoe Hare. *See* Hare, Snowshoe
Sorex
    cinereus, 20–21
    fumeus, 20–21
    hoyi, 20–21
    palustris, 20–21
Squirrels
    Gray, 30–31, *111, 112*
    Northern Flying, 34–35, *111*
    Red, 32–33, *111, 112*
    Southern Flying, 34–35, *111*
Stride, and half stride, 6, 8
Sylvilagus
    floridanus, 22–23
    transitionalis, 22–23
Symmetry, 5

Tamias striatus, 26–27, *111*
Tamiasciurus hudsonicus, 32–33, *111, 112*
Torpor, 27, 69
Trail Width, 7, 8

Urocyon cinereoargenteus, 64–65, *118, 119*
Ursus americana, 66–69

Vestigial toes, 7
Voles
    Meadow, 42–43
    Rock, 42–43
    S. Red-backed, 42–43
    Woodland or Pine, 42–43

Vulpes vulpes, 60–62, *118*

Wallows, 105, 107
Wapiti. *See* Elk
Weasels
    Long-tailed, 72–73, *120*
    Short-tailed or Ermine, 72–73
    Least, 72–73
Webbing, 37, 82, 83
Wolf, Gray, 54–57, *117*
    track patterns, 57
Woodchuck, 28–29

Zapus hudsonicus, 48–49